Casanova in London

Casanova in London

PETER QUENNELL

STEIN AND DAY/*Publishers*/New York

Acknowledgments

With a single exception, all these essays have appeared, often under a somewhat different shape, in various periodicals. For permission to reprint them, I am indebted to the editors of *Harper's Bazaar*, *Horizon*, *Life International*, the *London Magazine*, the *New Statesman*, the *New York Times*, the *Spectator*, and *The Times Literary Supplement*. I am also grateful to Messrs William Kimber & Company for leave to reprint my original introduction to Henry Mayhew's *London Labour and the London Poor*.

Peter Quennell
October 1970

First published in the United States of America 1971
Copyright © 1971 by Peter Quennell
Library of Congress Catalog Card No. 72-150603
All rights reserved
Printed in the United States of America
Stein and Day/*Publishers*/7 East 48 Street,
    New York, N.Y. 10017
SBN 8128-1368-5

Contents

Casanova in London

During the early summer of 1763, Jacques or Giacomo Casanova, who sometimes called himself the Chevalier de Seingalt, a native of Venice but also a citizen of Europe, well-known to the secret police of half a dozen different countries, decided he would visit England. Perhaps, after his recent successful exploitation of an elderly, crack-brained French noblewoman, the marquise d'Urfé, which may have brought him as much as a million francs, he preferred temporarily to leave Paris. Otherwise his motives were honest enough: he intended to promote in England, with the collaboration of the British government, an officially recognized public lottery of the kind that he had already run in France. And then, there was his natural restlessness. Like Ulysses, he felt that it was his destiny to explore 'the cities and the minds of men', while simultaneously he pursued his researches into the passions and the hearts of women.

At the time he was thirty-eight years old, a tall, swart, strongly-built personage, with bright dark eyes and an impressive beaked nose. In his youth, that enthusiastic collector of handsome men, Frederick the Great, had commented warmly on his fine appearance; and he was still full of energy, wit and charm – or so it seemed until he reached England. Then a sudden and disturbing change took place. . . . But, before we follow him across the Channel, something must be said about his character, more particularly about his true character in relation to his notorious legend. For 'Casanova' is one of the runaway names that have become dissociated from their original owner and indissolubly at-

I

tached to a certain type of human conduct. There can be no doubt that Casanova had earned his reputation as the indefatigable seducer of innumerable women; but his interests were far less specialized, and in some aspects far more altruistic, than those of the ordinary professional rake. He was versed in literature, devoted to learning, an amateur mathematician and scientist, who, between 1752 and 1798, published over a score of literary works, including some unsigned articles, very often on highly recondite topics. Among his chief English friends was Dr Maty, curator of the British Museum; and Maty introduced him to Samuel Johnson, with whom Casanova claimed to have discussed some absorbing etymological problems. His thirst for information was always unbounded; and it remained equally keen throughout his whole existence, whether he was studying the opposite sex, hobnobbing with famous literary men, or observing the habits and customs of an unfamiliar capital.

Yet, although it did not monopolize his whole attention, love, admittedly, was a subject to which he gave especial thought; and the maxims that stock his autobiography would provide the contents of a small volume. As a passport to amorous success, he recommends delicate, unremitting care: '. . . I knew that there is not a woman in the world who can resist the assiduous care and little attentions of a man who has determined he will win her love'; while, on a more scabrous level, he notes that very young women can often be seduced if a sister or a friend attends the seduction as an eye-witness. But conquest alone did not satisfy him: lovemaking must bring into play all his powers of appreciation; and in London he would refuse to entertain a beautiful and fashionable courtesan because he could not speak English, and Kitty Fisher had no foreign languages: 'Accustomed to love with all my senses, I could not abandon myself to love unless I employed my sense of hearing'.

Casanova was a greedily sensual man. But he was an adventurer who thought and felt, and whose ability to think and feel was intimately connected with even his grossest pleasures. Although he was superstitious, he had escaped a

2

sense of sin; and, though occasionally cruel, if it did not inter-
fere with his pursuit of amusement he was very often warm-
hearted. He possessed, moreover, an extremely valuable gift
– by merely desiring to do so, he could immediately fall in
love. Not all his affairs were genuine love affairs; but a surprisingly large number of his passing escapades would appear
to have bred that vital spark. If he were loved, he usually
loved in return, until the inevitable moment arrived when
he knew that it was time to say goodbye. Neither intentionally destructive, nor deliberately self-destructive, he was apt
to see his role as that of a genial Priapus in the Closed Garden
of eighteenth-century society, dispensing joy and, with it,
enlightenment, as he taught the women he encountered to
understand their own needs.

His autobiography, which he began to compose during the
last and saddest period of his life, at the Castle of Dux in
Bohemia, where he had been appointed honorary librarian
by its good-natured owner Count Waldstein, is both a record
and a testament – the story of the adventures he had lived
through and a summing up of his private beliefs and discoveries. This extraordinary and endlessly fascinating book
was still unfinished on his death; and, having remained in
manuscript for nearly thirty years, it was at length presented
to the reading public by the Dresden firm of Brockhaus. But
the German publisher did not choose to print it exactly as it
had been written, and enlisted the services of a Professor
Jean Laforgue, resident teacher of French at Dresden University. Laforgue was a remarkably unscrupulous editor. He
disliked Casanova's French style, which is lively and energetic, if often somewhat incorrect; and, while he prepared
the story for the press – the closing volume of the series appeared in 1838 – he allowed himself the widest latitude.

That Laforgue had taken serious liberties with Casanova's
text had long been known to every student of the memoirs.
But no disinterested reader had been permitted to examine
the manuscript; and we could not tell just how ruthlessly, or
how sympathetically, the professor had performed his func-
tion. At one moment, a rumour circulated that the precious

papers had been irrecoverably lost – perhaps burned in an Allied fire-raid, possibly abandoned and destroyed during the Russian invasion of East Germany. Happily, this rumour proved untrue. In 1964, from the archives of its first publishers who had since moved their offices to the West, Casanova's holograph emerged triumphant; and the authentic memoirs have now been published both in French and German; while Propylaen Verlag of Berlin and Munich have begun to issue a scholarly German translation.[1]

The effect is astonishing. Laforgue did not simply edit and amend; he rewrote and expanded whole episodes; wherever the reader casts his eye, there are traces of his ponderous academic touch. It was formerly believed that, besides editing, Laforgue had also bowdlerized Casanova's narrative. On the contrary, he proves to have enlarged and embellished some of the more obviously erotic scenes. The author's accounts of his amatory experiences are usually concise and vivid: the editor deliberately touches them up, adding here a word or two, and there a line, so as to invest the author's direct descriptions with a specious air of Gallic naughtiness. Laforgue's sense of decorum, however, would occasionally overcome his taste for licence; and, when Casanova, who was attracted to very young girls and not averse from the idea of incest, confesses that he had once thought of playing the Humbert Humbert with Sophie, the pretty little girl he believed to be his daughter, Laforgue takes a firm censorious stand and prudently cuts out the reference.

Seldom has a literary masterpiece received more brutal handling. Today, with the original text before us, we can see the superiority of Casanova's brisk Italianate French to Laforgue's pedestrian, but smooth-flowing prose. The memoirist was an accomplished storyteller; and his narrative gifts are especially apparent in the picture he draws of his calamitous visit to England. Everything about this strange country

---

[1] By Plon of Paris and Propylaen Verlag of Berlin and Munich. The present writer was privileged to contribute an introductory essay to the first two Propylaen volumes. From that introduction, which was translated into German, he has drawn some of the material incorporated in this study.

either puzzled or disconcerted him. The island named England, he wrote, had a colour that was all its own; 'the waters of the Thames have a different savour ... cattle, fish, whatever one eats, taste differently from what we eat abroad; horses are of a peculiar breed ... and men have a distinctive character.' England, he concluded, was a sea full of sandbanks; and those who sailed it should remember to be wary. On that wild and dangerous sea he was somehow taken off his guard, and swept into an amatory crisis through which he floundered like an inexperienced youth.

The beginning of September 1763 had marked a climacteric in his history. Never again was he to be quite the same man. As he reviewed those stormy, frustrating months, he felt that, on a certain calamitous autumn day, he had, in fact, begun to perish. 'It was on that fatal day ... that I began to die and ceased to live.' Looking back, he saw a process of gradual decline: the reverses he had undergone in London – 'which ended the first chapter of my life' – had led directly, through his final period in Venice – when he had earned a pittance as a government spy – to the miserable seclusion he endured at Dux, scribbling and yawning in Count Waldstein's library. He had now entered the third chapter, which could only end with death. 'The comedy will then have run its course. ... If the audience should chance to hiss, I very much hope that there will be nobody to bring me the news.'

Meanwhile, he could neither excuse his failure, nor find an explanation of its secret causes. Had he himself, conceivably, *willed* his downfall? Love was a notorious source of folly; and he was obliged to confess that he had loved beyond all reason. Casanova's biographer is equally mystified. He was still vigorous, well-provided with money, possessed an abounding personal charm, and had had a long experience in the management of women. On English soil, however, none of these powerful assets could save him from humiliation. ... Yet, the early stages of his visit showed Casanova in his most aggressive mood. Although the lottery scheme never materialized, owing to the unexpected removal of his chief supporter, he soon hired an expensive furnished house and, since English tavern fare was rich but unappetizing, engaged an admirable French cook. He spent his money in a judiciously prodigal manner. His Pall Mall residence alone cost him twenty pounds a week.

From this base Casanova proceeded to conduct three major amatory campaigns; of which the first and third were brilliantly successful, but the second ended in an ignominious rout. Each shows him under a different aspect. Thus his brief liaison with the aristocratic Portuguese girl whom he called Pauline X – o, but who is otherwise unidentifiable, reveals him as a tender, thoughtful and imaginative lover; his treatment of 'the Hanoverian women' – an impoverished widow and her five daughters, all of whom he presently enjoyed – displays him at his least attractive. He played on their fears, exploited their poverty and brutally swept aside their forlorn pretensions to virtue.

Between those episodes – one romantic and sentimental, the other harshly cynical – Casanova inserts a tragi-comic account of his association with La Charpillon and her family. At first sight, there was nothing to distinguish the seventeen-year-old Marianne Charpillon from a host of young women he had met and conquered. Her mother and grandmother, descendants of an honest Swiss pastor, had both been minor *demi-mondaines*, listed in the secret archives of the French police; and, while they were living abroad, Casanova had already met them. They had since left Paris and settled down at a modest house in Denmark Street, Soho, whither their confederates, a gang of petty cardsharpers, lured the victims whom they meant to pluck. The Charpillons had many acquaintances among the alien population of the City; and it was M. Malignan, a Flemish soldier of fortune, who presented the Italian tourist to Madame Charpillon and her daughter.

Marianne Charpillon at once aroused his cupidity, which presently merged into a much deeper feeling; for not only was she witty and seductive, but to a sharp mind and engaging manners she added conspicuous physical attractions. She was, indeed, he thought, a great beauty, with light chestnut hair, azure eyes, a dazzlingly white skin, small but perfectly

6

formed breasts, long dimpled hands and tiny feet. 'Her physiognomy [he wrote], which was gentle and candid-looking, suggested a soul notable for delicacy of sentiment'; and she possessed, moreover, that air of distinction which is usually associated with patrician birth. Here Nature lied, says Casanova bitterly. She was neither delicate nor well-bred: 'This girl had conceived the plan of making me wretched even before she had learned to know me; and, what is more, she told me so.'

The story of Casanova's sufferings is a fantastic record of folly and deceit – all the more bizarre because he had embarked on the episode without illusions. He knew the family and had had an opportunity of observing at least one of their associates – the Frenchman Ange Goudar, whom he describes as a pimp and a cardsharper, a police spy and a perjured witness. Considering his wide experience of life, and the knowledge it had brought him of adventurers and tricksters – he was acquainted, he once declared, with every vagrant adventurer on earth – Casanova, in a more lucid and less impassioned mood, might very well have come off scot-free. But he did not allow for La Charpillon's natural talents – her knack both of exploiting his passions and of discovering his weakest points, the gift she possessed of plunging her sting into some unprotected nerve centre, then half resuscitating her almost paralyzed victim, only to expose him to fresh displays of cruelty.

Why was Casanova the victim she chose? That is a question we cannot fully answer. He had money: he was notably generous: he could afford, and was prepared to pay, her price. La Charpillon was not an innocent girl, but had already been kept by the Venetian envoy and, no doubt, by several other men. She had much to gain, and little to lose, if she granted Casanova what he sought; while the course of action she preferred to pursue involved her in many real dangers. Admitted to her bed but refused her embraces, her suitor grew extremely violent. On one occasion he bruised her severely, and tore the shift that she was wearing 'right down to the small of her back'. Nothing could shake her infernal obstinacy. 'Cruel night, desolating night, during which I appealed to the monster in every tone I could command: gentleness, anger, reason, remonstrances, threats, rage, despair, petitions, tears, ignominy and appalling insults. For three whole hours she resisted me; and, all that time, she never breathed a word. . . .' Finally, bewildered, stupefied, his brain on fire, Casanova dressed in the dark and wandered home.

Soon he felt that he must be going mad: 'I think the natural outcome of a long period of self-contempt is a state of despair that leads to suicide.' A professed libertine, he had been untrue to his creed, to the duty that he owed himself. He had shown irresolution, ridiculous timidity: 'That morning (he remembered) in a timid voice I asked her if she meant to spend the night with me. . . .' He had allowed his senses to inflame his heart, and his heart to rule his head. Meanwhile, Goudar, the expert pimp, was hurrying busily to and fro. He pretended to sympathize with Casanova's misfortunes, and at one moment suggested that his friend should overcome Charpillon's resistance by persuading her to sit down in a specially contrived chair, an ingenious piece of mechanism that would thereupon imprison her limbs and leave her at her lover's mercy.

Such a chair he thoughtfully offered to purchase. Casanova refused: rape in England, he knew, was a hanging crime; and he still hoped that persuasion might succeed. There he was wrong: La Charpillon's numerous triumphs seemed merely to increase her malice. Arriving unexpectedly at the house in Denmark Street, he found his idol and a handsome young barber's assistant stretched out on a sofa and enjoyably 'making the beast with two backs' – the expressive phrase that the book-loving amorist had borrowed from the works of Shakespeare. He then set about and thrashed his rival, broke every chair in the sitting room, and demolished a looking glass and a valuable porcelain service that had been his own presents. La Charpillon escaped into the street; and the next day he heard that she was seriously ill.

This was shortly followed by the news that she was expected to die within an hour's time. 'I felt, at that moment, as it were an icy hand crushing my heart'; and he promptly determined to commit suicide, loaded his pockets with lead shot and trudged off doggedly towards the river. 'A human being,' he notes, 'very easily goes mad.' His mind had always included a hidden germ of superstition; and he was convinced that 'in irrecoverably decisive actions we are only masters of ourselves up to a certain point.' Half way across Westminster Bridge, whom should he meet but Mr Agar, a rich and good-natured young Englishman, capable of providing just the diversion that he needed! They drank together at a tavern with a pair of friendly girls; and, although Casanova found that he had not the slightest appetite for roast beef and pudding, or, indeed, for making love, the debauch that ensued had a temporarily palliative effect. That same night, however, they visited Ranelagh Gardens, where, on the dance-floor, he caught sight of La Charpillon performing with her usual elegance; at which Casanova broke out into an icy sweat, and a convulsive tremor shook his arms.

Now that he had avoided death, he slowly and painfully recovered; but he had not yet escaped from La Charpillon's fury. On his plea, her mother and her aunt were arrested as swindlers and consigned to gaol; but he himself was hauled before the blind magistrate Sir John Fielding, half-brother of the novelist Henry Fielding, and accused of having scarred her face. Without much difficulty he managed to regain his freedom. But his thirst for revenge was still unsatisfied; and he devised the ridiculous expedient of purchasing a young parrot, which he taught to repeat 'Miss Charpillon is even more of a harlot than her mother!', and then disposed of on the public market.

It was an absurdly undignified stratagem; and he could not forget that his failure to seduce La Charpillon had cost him at least a thousand pounds. Although his conquest of 'the Hanoverian women' did something to console his self-esteem, that, too, was a somewhat expensive business; and, after nine months spent in England, he became aware that he was running short of money. At this unhappy juncture, he negotiated a worthless bill of exchange, which he had accepted against a gambling debt, with an unsuspicious City banker. If prosecuted, he was in danger of being hanged. But Casanova had never been afraid to cut his losses; and, leaving his shirts behind – they were immediately stolen by his trusted negro servant – he packed his trunks and made a bolt for Paris.

Clearly, he had had enough of England. He had found the spectacle of London life more instructive than amusing. The English, he decided, were a rough, unruly race: and the boisterous urban mob especially delighted in tormenting foreigners, particularly those who wore Parisian bag wigs. Even the newspapers took outrageous liberties: 'the freedom of the press leads to remarkable abuses.' As to English merchants, at the Royal Exchange a man was known by the size of his income, not by his name or his reputation for honesty. ... Altogether, the drama that had brought to an end the first chapter of his life history had had a somewhat ominous background. Like William Hickey, another daring rake and accomplished self-portraitist, Casanova possessed an extraordinary memory, what is nowadays known as the gift of 'total recall'. London he remembered with unusually strong feelings. The year 1763 had been a watershed in his existence; and from that watershed he had slowly descended into the deserts of a lonely and neglected old age.

The library at Dux was evidently his final refuge; but the admission must have cost him dear. His host Count Waldstein was kind and hospitable; yet he often seemed a trifle negligent. The Count's servants were lazy and inattentive; Casanova grew tyrannical and peevish. 'There was not a day (writes the Prince de Ligne) in which, whether for his coffee, his milk, the macaroni he demanded, there was not a quarrel. ... Dogs had barked during the night; an unexpected number of guests had forced him to eat at a side table. ... The priest had annoyed him by trying to convert him. The Count had not been the first to greet him with a good morning. ... He had become angry; they had laughed. He had gesticulated declaiming Italian verses; they had laughed. He had made, on entering a room, the bow taught him by Marcel, the famous dancing master sixty years before; they had laughed. ... He had dressed up with his white plume, his suit of gold-embroidered silk, his waistcoat of black velvet and his garters of rhinestone buckles on his silk stockings; they had laughed. . . .' All these humiliations could ultimately be traced back to the supreme humiliation he had undergone during the year 1763. The vindictive laughter of La Charpillon, adorable, abominable, unforgettable girl, still resounded in his septua` genarian ears.

Crusoe's Island

The Selcraigs were one of those families who thrive in an atmosphere of strife and discord. They scandalized their Scottish neighbours; they defied authority; with even greater enthusiasm, they wrangled and fought among themselves. Pitched battles were apt to occur upon the smallest provocation. Late in the year 1701, for instance, Andrew Selcraig having carried home a 'can full of salt water,' his brother Alexander 'did take a drink through mistake'; and, when Andrew laughed at the face he pulled, Alexander began to beat him; whereupon Andrew rushed out of the house to fetch an elder brother John, while their determined father squatted with his back to the door, meaning, he afterward explained, to prevent Alexander from going 'to get down his pistol'. John's wife, Margaret, then joined in, assaulted 'the said Alexander,' who was grappling with both his father and her husband, and, before she was finally bundled into the street, denounced him as a 'false loon'.

This domestic hubbub attracted the attention of the Kirk elders; and, on November 30, Alexander Selcraig, 'according to the session's appointment, appeared before the pulpit, and made acknowledgment of his sin. . . .' It was not his first offence. Six years earlier, at the age of nineteen, he had received a public rebuke 'for his undecent behaviour in the church'. But by now he had evidently had enough of his father and the noisy Selcraig household; and sometime in 1702 he said good-bye to Largo, the small Scottish seaport where the elder Selcraig carried on his business as a shoemaker and tanner, and enlisted under an English sea captain who was manning an expedition to the South Seas. Alexander Selcraig, presently renamed Selkirk, must already have served his apprenticeship at sea, though exactly how and where we cannot tell. For, when he enlisted under Captain William Dampier, the renowned ex-pirate and circumnavigator of the globe, he was appointed sailing master of the galley *Cinque Ports,* a vessel of one hundred and twenty tons which was to accompany the *St George,* commanded by Captain Dampier himself.

Thus Selkirk exchanged the squalid confusion of his life at home for the anarchic rigours of a life at sea. The white-winged sailing ship is an imaginative symbol of freedom; during the days of sail, it was more often an inferno of misery and discontent. Below decks there was scarcely room to turn; the food was abominable and, after a long diet of salt-beef and biscuit, men began to rot with scurvy. On ships of the line, savage physical punishments helped to maintain law and order. The ship on which Selkirk had embarked was a petty privateer, one of those vessels which, in times of war, were fitted out to act as licensed pirates, encouraged to harry French and Spanish craft and now and then take by surprise and plunder an ill-defended Spanish settlement.

Dampier's expedition was somewhat unsuccessful; and soon his men were grumbling and his officers quarrelling. Naturally Selkirk was a major disputant. Early in 1704 the *Cinque Ports* reached the island of Juan Fernandez, or Más a Tierra, a stark mountainous volcanic ridge, more than ten miles long and nearly four miles broad, lying about four hundred miles off what is now the coast of Chile. There, Selkirk and forty-one other men announced that they would no longer serve under their incompetent captain, Thomas Stradling, and Selkirk led them ashore, where they organized a kind of sitdown strike. It took all Dampier's powers of persuasion to get them back again. But the expedition continued to go badly; and, in May, 1704, the *St George* and the *Cinque Ports* decided to take different courses.

That autumn, the roving *Cinque Ports* returned to the shelter of Juan Fernandez. The captain and the sailing master were still at odds. Stradling, his subordinate claimed, was a bungler who did not know his trade; and, when the Captain proposed to set sail, Selkirk refused to accompany him and insisted that he and everything he owned should at once be put ashore. This was a serious error of judgment; none of his companions followed. It is said that Selkirk lost heart, tried to rejoin the party, and splashed out after them across the shallows. But he was too late; and he stood there alone, knee-deep in the swirling surf. He shouted after his faithless friends; he expostulated, implored and argued. The ship's boat gradually drew away; behind him rose the dense green thickets and steep grey precipices of a wild unpeopled island. As the *Cinque Ports* hoisted her sails, he dropped headlong into a deep, apalling solitude.

Loneliness is a theme that has always fascinated the literary imagination. Man is born alone and dies alone; he lives alone amid his secret thoughts and feelings. Selkirk's plight typifies the human condition at its most defenceless and its most unfriended. He was a man thrown back on his own resources, Shakespeare's 'poor forked animal' stripped of the armour of civilized existence with which we enclose the naked human organism. He had rejected authority, challenged society; now he had to face himself.

His first reaction was one of passionate despair, accompanied by a thrilling sense of terror. He did not sleep until exhaustion closed his eyes, and seldom ate 'till Hunger constrain'd him, partly for grief, and partly for want of Bread and Salt'. In his solitude he remembered his childhood training; the riotous young man, whose 'undecent behaviour' had so offended the elders of the Kirk, thumbed through his family Bible, prayed aloud, and sang psalms. Then, little by little, the natural man prevailed; he was strong, resourceful, and resilient. His island was no barren rock: 'the broken craggy precipices which had appeared so unpromising at a distance,' wrote Commander George Anson, an Englishman who visited the island in 1741, 'were covered with woods, and between them were interspersed the finest vallies clothed with most beautiful verdure, watered with numerous streams and cascades of clear water.' He had his musket with him and a bag of gunpowder, 'a Hatchet, a Knife, a Kettle ... some practical Pieces, and his Mathematical Instruments and Books.' Before long he had built 'two Hutts with Piemento Trees, cover'd them with long Grass, and lin'd them with the Skins of Goats, which he kill'd with his Gun as he wanted. . . .'

When his powder eventually ran out, he learned to chase the goats on foot. Scottish children of his class and period very seldom wore shoes; and Selkirk became a barefooted hunter, capable of outdistancing most of the animals he chased. Juan Fernandez at the time abounded in goats which, together with cats and rats, had been established there by previous colonists. The rats were troublesome; they gnawed his horny feet and chewed holes in his precious garments. In order 'to defend him against them he fed and tamed Numbers of young Kitlings, who lay about his Bed, and preserved him from the Enemy.'

Even the 'Monsters of the Deep' – fur seals and elephant seals – whose 'dreadful Howlings ... seemed too terrible to be made for human Ears,' ceased to alarm him as he lay awake at night. He dared to approach the slow and stolid creatures, and presently discovered how to kill them 'with greatest Ease imaginable'. He also caught turtles and crayfish, and plucked the fruit of the pimento trees (thought to have been sandalwood, which has now completely vanished from the island), the leaves of an edible palm, which he called the cabbage tree, and the excellent English turnips that Captain Dampier's crew had planted. The pimento trees provided stores of sweetly fragrant firewood. Surrounded by some hundreds of amiable cats and a troop of domesticated kids, he led a sober, patriarchal life. Frequently he would sing and dance among his purring, capering household: 'so that by the Care of Providence and Vigour of his Youth, being now but about thirty years old, he came at last to conquer all the Inconveniences of his Solitude. . . .'

His worst adventure occurred when, pursuing a goat, he fell over an unsuspected precipice and lay stunned and wounded a day and a night, the body of the dead goat awkwardly doubled up beneath him. But once more he rallied; he managed to deal with his bodily hurts and ills as efficiently as he had cured his spiritual disorder, and even made good use of the native 'black Pepper call'd *Malagita*, which was very good to expel Wind, and against Griping of the Guts.'

Yet the longing for human company persisted – almost any company but that of the Spaniards; for the War of the Spanish Succession had been raging since 1701. Several ships passed the island like ghosts, 'but only two came in to achor.' When Selkirk ran down from his lookout, he recognized a Spanish landing party and had to retreat into the recesses of the island; upon which they fired their guns and gave chase. Once he climbed to the topmost branches of a tree, 'at the foot of which they made water, and kill'd several Goats just by, but went off again without discovering him.'

At last deliverance came. Toward the end of January, 1709, when Selkirk's solitary reign had lasted four years and four months, a couple of English privateers, the *Duke* and the *Duchess*, commanded by Captain Woodes Rogers, with William Dampier aboard as pilot, approached the rocky shores of Juan Fernandez. They were alarmed by a distant mysterious light; and, although they were eager to leave their vessels – many of the crew were suffering from scurvy – not until the second of February were they resolute enough to send 'our Yall ashore'. Their alarm soon proved groundless; 'all this stir and apprehension arose, as we afterwards found, for one poor naked Man. . . .' Not that Selkirk was literally naked; he still possessed a single shirt, and was otherwise warmly clad in goatskins. Nor was his condition really pitiable. Although 'at first coming on board us, he had so much forgot his Language for want of Use, that we could scarce understand him,' he was sound in mind and body. 'Exercise of walking and running' had long ago 'clear'd him of all gross Humours.' Like most eighteenth-century seamen, Selkirk must have been a hard drinker; but, on this occasion, when 'we offer'd him a Dram . . . he would not touch it . . . and 'twas some time before he could relish our victuals.'

Selkirk's subsequent adventures were relatively commonplace. On the voyage home, he helped to attack and plunder the Peruvian settlement of Guyaquil; and he returned to England having accumulated some £800 in prize money. Once he had reverted to so-called civilized life, he underwent a gradual change. Richard Steele, who interviewed him in 1713, reported that when they first met, 'there was a strong but cheerful seriousness in his look, and a certain disregard to the ordinary things about him, as if he had been sunk in thought'; but after only a few months, 'I could not recollect that I had seen him; familiar discourse in this town had taken off the loneliness of his aspect, and quite altered the air of his face.' His violent temper again declared itself; at Bristol, in 1713, he was charged with assaulting one 'Richard Nettle, shipwright'. He would appear also to have become an unscrupulous philanderer; in 1716 he carried off to London a Scottish farmer's daughter named Sophia Bruce and, she claimed, made her his legal wife. But soon afterwards he joined the Royal Navy, and then, during a spell of shore leave, in December, 1720, he married a widow, Frances Candish, or Candis, who kept a public house near Plymouth. In 1721 Selkirk died at sea, struck down by a deadly tropical fever.

Meanwhile he had enjoyed his moment of fame. Woodes Roger's story of his travels, *A Cruising Voyage round the World*, which included the fullest account of Selkirk's experiences, was originally published in the year 1712; and in December 1713 Steele wrote up his interview with Selkirk as a literary essay for *The Englishman*. Steele was a practised journalist and a shrewd contemporary moralist. He described Selkirk's struggle against dark and self-destructive impulses, explained how he had conquered his dejection 'by the Force of Reason, and frequent reading of the Scriptures,' painted the idyllic life he had led, once his fears and miseries had been thrust behind him, and concluded by declaring that 'this plain Man's Story is a memorable Example, that he is happiest who confines his Wants to natural Necessities' and never seeks to go beyond them. The way was now open for Daniel Defoe, whose *Life and Strange Surprizing Adventures of*

18

Robinson Crusoe of York, Mariner reached the world in 1719.

It seems unlikely that Defoe had met Selkirk; and for his imaginative record of travel, Rogers and Steele were not his only sources. In Dampier's *Voyages* he had read of the Indian castaway, Will, who, at the end of the seventeenth century, had passed two lonely years on Selkirk's island; and he may perhaps have consulted a recent English translation of an extremely curious Arabic volume, *The Improvement of Human Reason exhibited in the Life of Ebn Yokdan*,[1] a Muslim castaway who overcomes his surroundings and in solitude obtains an intuitive knowledge of God. Daniel Defoe was an experienced salesman of his work; and travellers' tales were particularly popular at the beginning of the eighteenth century. He was anxious to produce a book that would sell; as a theorist and an artist, he was keenly excited by the subject of Richard Steele's essay. Selkirk had conquered 'by force of reason'; throughout his life Defoe, too, endeavoured to apply reason – sound, practical, middle-class commonsense – to a large variety of current problems.

Thus the island he described became the microcosm of an island commonwealth. Nature had stocked it for the use of Man. How should Man employ those riches, hampered, as he so often was, by the bonds of ignorance and fear and greed? *Robinson Crusoe* is a picture of Reason triumphant; such is the story's universal aspect. On another plane, Defoe, who had dabbled in a scheme for colonizing the South Seas, was deeply interested in the problems of modern colonial expansion; and Crusoe's island is the pattern for a colony close to the shores of the South American continent, a region toward which English merchants and 'projectors' were then turning greedy, speculative eyes. Defoe's book shows a middle-class Englishman – just such an Englishman as he was himself – in the role of imperial colonist and benevolent administrator.

Robinson Crusoe, the author's first novel, was written and published in 1719, when he was almost sixty. But that year Defoe is thought to have fathered more than two hundred

[1] See R. L. Mégroz, *The Real Robinson Crusoe* (1939), a study of Selkirk which is particularly interesting on the subject of his early life.

and ninety printed works, none of them downright fiction, but covering an enormous range of subjects. His career, like Crusoe's, had been varied. He had dealt in stockings; manufactured bricks and tiles; travelled up and down the country in search of political and commercial information; produced pamphlets on behalf of the Tory government; and, more recently, after the Tories had fallen, had undertaken to support the Whigs by posing as a Tory journalist and, in that rôle, doing his best to 'disable and enervate' the publications of High Tory writers. Once he had been imprisoned and pilloried, but, owing to his clever conduct of the situation, had been pelted with flowers instead of filth and stones.

Meanwhile Defoe had continued to float and abandon endless schemes of self-enrichment, including a scheme to make a corner in civet, the basic material used by the manufacturers of scent. When it failed, he was left with a breeding stock of seventy unwanted civet cats. He had married an heiress, but in 1692 had gone bankrupt, with debts amounting to £17,000, in those days a very considerable sum. During the process he had begotten eight children, whose future caused him grave disquiet; and he was now living among his family in a large old-fashioned house at Stoke Newington. His debts, however, still disturbed him; and he often found it expedient to retire into secret London lodgings.

Few writers have been more extraordinarily industrious. For Defoe, to draw breath was to write and publish; and *Robinson Crusoe*, once he had set his hand to it, seems to have been composed at breakneck speed. The year 1719 was his *annus mirabilis*; it was then that he emerged as a master of the modern art of storytelling. His novel achieved an immediate success; but he did not rest upon his laurels. In 1720, besides continuing *Robinson Crusoe*, whose *Serious Reflections* were now presented to the literary public, he published *Life and Adventures of Mr Duncan Campbell* and *Captain Singleton*; in 1722, the immortal *Moll Flanders*, *A Journal of the Plague Year*, and *Colonel Jack*; in 1724, *The Fortunate Mistress*. All these books had admirable qualities; but from the point of view of the common reader, *Robinson Crusoe* remains the novelist's unchallenged masterpiece. Its fame spread through the whole of Europe. Even the captious Jean-Jacques Rousseau was to recommend it, in *Emile*, as the best of educational textbooks.

Yet the world-wide celebrity of *Robinson Crusoe* rests upon a single episode, which, in the ninteenth-century edition before me, occupies only 244 out of 607 pages. Though Crusoe's intrepid voyages across the wilds of China and Siberia are almost as exciting and well described, no one pays them much heed. It is the island story that holds our attention. The island, like the sailing ship, is a powerfully poetic image, which symbolizes both freedom and loneliness; for on an island Man is at once the undisputed master of his surroundings and the isolated victim of his own destiny. The story delights children as much as it interests the adult critic: Defoe appeals to the child in man and to the adult who lies hidden in the child. Every child has built huts and bonfires, has pretended to beat off a host of savages, and has reigned supreme over a troop of friendly animals. But the imaginative child is also naturally creative; and *Robinson Crusoe* is the description of a man planning and creating an entire new world. He is not only the original exponent of self-help, the type of proud suburban householder who embellishes his kitchen or constructs a garden shed; he is the artist, too, and finds the act of creation deeply absorbing and uplifting. Take Crusoe's famous account of how he manages to fire an earthen vessel:

I had no Notion of a Kiln, such as the Potters burn in . . . but I plac'd three large Pipkins, and two or three Pots in a Pile one upon another, and plac'd my Fire-wood all round it with a great Heap of Embers under them; I ply'd the Fire with fresh Fuel . . . till I saw the Pots in the inside red hot quite thro', and observ'd that they did not crack at all . . . so I slack'd my Fire gradually, till the Pots began to abate of the red Colour, and watching them all Night, that I might not let the Fire abate too fast, in the Morning I had three very good, I will not say handsome, Pipkins; and two other Earthern Pots, as hard burnt as cou'd be desir'd . . . No Joy at a Thing of so mean a Nature was ever equal to mine, when I found I had made an Earthern

Pot that would bear the Fire; and I had hardly Patience to stay till they were cold, before I set one upon the Fire again ... to boil me some Meat, which it did admirably well.

Defoe's method of writing is as plain and practical as Crusoe's method of furnishing his house. Both were plain men. Although Crusoe wanders around the globe – just as Defoe had explored modern England, from Newgate Gaol to the statesman's cabinet and the anterooms of the British Court itself – in the end, after 'a life of infinite variety,' he reverts to the sober middle class station, the 'middle state' that, when he was still young and restless, his ancient father had so often praised:

He ask'd me what Reasons more than a meer wand'ring Inclination I had had for leaving my Father's House and my native Country ... He told me it was for Men of desperate Fortunes on one Hand, or of aspiring, superior Fortunes on the other ... to rise by Enterprize, and make themselves famous in Undertakings of a Nature out of the common Road; that these things were all either too far above me, or too far below me; that mine was the middle State, or what might be called the upper Station of *Low Life*, which he had found by long Experience was the best State in the World ... not exposed to the Miseries and Hardships, the Labour and Sufferings of the mechanick Part of Mankind, and not embarrass'd with the Pride, Luxury, Ambition and Envy of the upper part of Mankind.

Defoe, however, could no more follow his own precepts than Crusoe could obey his father's counsels. He was an exceptional man, an artist in spite of himself; and, in its own way, the style he developed has very seldom been improved on. *Robinson Crusoe* and *Moll Flanders* each purport to tell a plain, unvarnished story; but into his narrative Defoe is perpetually slipping some revelatory detail or dramatic image. He might try to write like an honest, straightforward trades-man; he could not help seeing and feeling like an artist, and recording what he saw – he had an exquisite gift of observation – with an imaginative artist's skill and delicacy. When Crusoe is first cast up on his island, he thinks of his comrades who have perished in the storm: 'as for them, I never saw them afterwards, or any Sign of them, except three of their Hats, one Cap, and two Shoes that were not Fellows.'

It is the last detail that accents the whole passage; the fact that the shoes he picks up are 'not fellows' strengthens his increasing sense of solitude. Similarly, the terrors that sometimes beset him are epitomized in the story of the 'monstrous frightful old He-goat', whose 'two broad shining Eyes' gleam out at him from the dusky hollow of a cave, and whose death rattle – 'a very loud Sigh, like that of a Man in some Pain . . . follow'd by a broken Noise, as if of Words half express'd, and then a deep Sigh again' – brings Crusoe to a sudden standstill and makes him sweat with fear.

The description of a single footprint he finds in the sand is one of those passages in European literature that have left a permanent mark upon the human memory – symbolic scenes that seem to transcend fiction and to become a part of life itself. Once more Crusoe is terrified: 'after innumerable fluttering Thoughts, like a man perfectly confus'd . . . I came Home to my Fortification . . . terrify'd to the last Degree, looking behind me at every two or three Steps. . . .' Such an adventure never happened to Selkirk; and it is interesting to see how the novelist, while making the most of the material on which his story was based, has transfigured and enlarged his theme.

Crusoe, too, has been a sinner and a wanderer, enveloped in 'a certain stupidity of Soul, without desire of good or conscience of Evil'; but, unlike Selkirk, who, after he had been released from his island, soon drifted back into his old courses, he is a highly sensitive and well-organized man, possessing a remarkable capacity for self-discipline. To call Alexander Selkirk 'the real Crusoe' is to misunderstand the nature of the artist's business. The true artist must always adapt; he reshapes a theme to suit his private purposes. Defoe, who shifted Selkirk's island from the South Pacific toward 'the Mouth of the Great River of Orinoco' and condemned Crusoe to an imprisonment of 'eight and twenty years,' whereas his 'real' counterpart had suffered only four years and four months, took everything that was memorable in the personality of Alexander Selkirk and, blending it with much that was memorable in himself, formed the full-length portrait of a modern hero.

The Goncourts

I was once unwise enough to submit to an appendicectomy without a general anaesthetic; and, as I lay on the operating table, my view of the ominous preparations only obstructed by a narrow strip of canvas, I noticed that the entire scene – masked surgeon and nurses and their glittering instruments – was mirrored by the glass of a large lamp suspended just above my head. 'If I were Jules or Edmond de Goncourt,' I thought, 'here is an opportunity that I should welcome. What a page it would have made for their *Journal* – the ceremony of a modern operation, observed, moment by moment, through the eyes of the chief sufferer! But then, I am *not* one of the Goncourts,' I concluded hastily, and croaked out an urgent request that the too revelatory lamp might be tilted at another angle.

Nevertheless, there had been an instant of hestitation; for I was reading the Goncourts at the time; and, while a reader is still deep in the *Journal*, their influence is extremely strong. So exclusive a devotion to literature cannot fail to command our respect. Perhaps the Goncourts were right in the end: that to the gift of imagination a novelist should do his best to add the faculty of scientific observation: that he must seize every opportunity of documenting himself upon the life of his period, constantly amassing notes irrespective of their immediate value, storing up a squirrel-hoard of facts from which he can presently draw the rough material for a striking and illuminating passage. Not until one examines the novels that resulted does it become clear that the Goncourts' system must, in some respects, have been at fault. With the possible exception of *Germinie Lacerteux*, all the narratives on which they expended such immense labour seem unexpectedly lifeless and artificial. The documentation, of course, is impressive; but the interesting facts they have assembled do not form a living whole: beneath the stylistic skin that clothes the framework of fact we can usually detect a certain hollowness and deadness.

Incidentally, if their method was misguided – first they collected the information; the imagination needed to transfigure it was called in at a secondary stage – they themselves, as creative writers, were considerably hampered by their personal temperament. Their egotism, personal and professional – *l'égoïsme dans la fraternité* – always separated them from the world they studied. They sympathized in so far as they could – no one could have *tried* harder to see life from the point of view of an uninstructed working girl. But they extended sympathy and invoked compassion rather with the air of performing a deliberate act of faith.

Most artists are both selfish and sensitive; but, to make the Goncourts' case more difficult, every failing they possessed was inevitably multiplied by two. Although Jules is said to have been expansive and mercurial, whereas Edmond, the elder, was somewhat reserved and saturnine, such was the strength of the fraternal bond that each, far from counterbalancing, helped to reinforce the other's tendencies. Thus they were doubly irritable, doubly suspicious, doubly determined to succeed at any cost. Neither of them was a warm-hearted man; and there were moments, one cannot help feeling, when collectively they became a monster, a twin-headed dragon of wrath and arrogance, furiously poised to strike. In his excellent biography,[1] M. André Billy, although himself a member of the Académie Goncourt, makes no attempt to disguise the founding fathers' weaknesses. He points out, for example, in a particularly interesting chapter, how few of the friends whom they pretended to respect and love were spared savage castigation once, behind closed doors, they had settled

[1] André Billy, *Les Frères Goncourt*. La vie littèraire à Paris pendant la seconde moitié du XIXe siècle. Flammarion, 1954.

26

down to write their *Journal*. Flaubert did not escape; nor did
Gautier and Sainte-Beuve. As for the greatest poet of his
generation, they did not deny that Baudelaire's pen, like their
own, was 'entirely devoted to art'; but they were repelled
both by his appearance and by his private mannerisms. Had
he not once inhabited a small hotel, in the immediate neighbourhood of a railway station, where his bedroom gave on to
a busy passage, and he was accustomed to sit with his door
wide open, affording to every passer by the spectacle of himself at work, '*en application de génie, les mains fouillant sa
pensée à travers ses longs cheveux blancs*'? Baudelaire's eccentric dandyism, at a time when he had decided to cut his
hair, is the subject of another note: '*Il est sans cravate, le col
nu, la tête rasée, en vrai toilette de guillotiné*', they remarked after encountering him at the Café Riche. '. . . *de
petites mains, lavées, écurées, soignées commes des mains
de femme – et avec cela une tête de maniaque, une voix
coupante comme une voix d'acier, et une élocution visant
à la précision ornée d'un Saint-Just. . . .*' But the epitaph
they composed was most damning of all. '*J'inclinerais à croire*
(observed Jules, little forseeing, as M. Billy remarks, that,
only eighteen months later, he himself was destined to die
insane) *que la folie n'attaque pas les grandes volontés, les
grands talents. Elle n'atteint . . . qu'un Baudelaire, c'est-à-
dire un Prudhomme exaspéré, un bourgeois qui s'est tour-
menté toute sa vie pour se donner l'élégance de paraître
fou. Il s'y est si bien appliqué et tendu qu'il est mort idiot!*'
Whereas Baudelaire was a tormented and distorted bourgeois, they themselves were aristocrats. This is a description
that has been adopted by many of their critics and by their
present biographer, M. Billy. But, at any rate in the literal
meaning of the term, their claims to aristocracy were
extremely tenuous, their great-grandfather having been an
advocate and notary who, three years before the Revolution,
had purchased a small property named Goncourt and acquired the title that went with it, '*seigneur de Noncourt et de
Goncourt*'. Despite the *particule nobiliaire*, at least on their
father's side they were the offspring of worthy middle class

stock; and from that source they derived their modest but sufficient income. It was never their misfortune to be obliged to write for a living: glory was their sole object. Passionately conscientious artists, who would spare no pains to satisfy their own exacting private literary standards, they were also intensely ambitious, bent on carving out a public career. Even weekly journalism had not been neglected: *'Chaque matin éveiller Paris avec son idée! Tous les jours battre la charge ... tenir la France suspendue à sa plume! La lutte, la lutte quotidienne! ... La guerre de la tête, enfin! Ah! les belles fatigues!'*

Pleasure itself – although they allowed pleasure its due – was subordinated to their exhausting plan of campaign. The love affairs in which they indulged were generally prosaic and brief – *'l'amour* (they wrote proudly) *nous prend cinq heures par semaine, de dix à onze, et pas une pensée avant ou après'*; and they seem to have been happiest when they had fixed their attention upon an amiable midwife named Maria – *'une grosse femme, les cheveux blonds, crespelés et relevées autour du front'* – whose professional confidences were as interesting as a book by Dr Baudeloque, and the dimples of whose voluptuous behind recalled a divinity by François Boucher. Edmond and Jules shared her affections; but, although they appreciated the splendour of her body – *'l'ampleur et la majesté d'une fille de Rubens'* – and the gaiety and generosity of her happy proletarian nature, she would appear to have been chiefly valuable to them as a teller of surprising stories. It fell to Maria's lot, after the sudden death of their apparently faithful maidservant Rose, who, for twenty-five years, almost every night of their lives, had tucked the brothers up in bed, to open their eyes to Rose's secret life and explain that she had been a hardened thief, an inveterate drunkard and a nymphomaniac – the revelation that inspired their finest novel, *Germinie Lacerteux*.

There they came close to succeeding in fiction; but neither *Germinie Lacerteux* nor the series of critical volumes, in which they expressed their discerning taste for Japanese art and for the exquisite civilization of the eighteenth century, can rival the *Journal* as a work of literature. True, the *Journal* itself has a displeasing and disappointing side; for it lacks the element of relief that might have been provided by writers whose emotional range was less restricted. At times, indeed, the authors' comments may strike us as astonishingly foolish. Thus, towards the end of March 1858, they paid a visit – apparently it was their first – to the animals in the Jardin des Plantes, watched a snake swallowing a frog and saw the hippopotamus *'ouvrant, à fleur d'eau, cette chose rose et immense et informe, cette bouche ressemblant à un lotus gigantesque fait de muqueuses. . . .'* But the beauty and oddity and immense diversity of the animal kingdom was dismissed by these literary visitors with a light and passing sneer. The Grand Designer showed little aesthetic sense: *'Peu de dépense d'imagination de la part du Créateur. Beaucoup trop de répétitions de formes chez les animaux. . . .'*

It is a lonely world that the Goncourts seem to inhabit, as one by one the friends they had been prepared to admire prove unworthy of their serious regard and shrink away into the background. A single hero remains on the stage – their old friend, the draughtsman and social commentator, Sulpice-Guillaume Chevalier, better known to the world under his pseudonym Gavarni. Him they would never cease to respect and love. Eighteen years older than Edmond, who had been born in 1822, he soon acquired in their existence the authority of a parental sage. He, too, was lonely by nature and perhaps not overburdened with the ordinary human feelings. In his youth a conquering dandy, passionately addicted to the pursuit of women – a hobby that he called 'the classification of butterflies' – Gavarni admitted, in later life, that the only human creatures he had ever genuinely loved were his old parents and his two children.

The hero of innumerable Opera Balls, for which he had designed a long series of exquisite and fantastic costumes, the unsuccessful editor of *Le Journal des Gens du Monde*, a fashion magazine in which the fashions he had himself designed were illustrated by his own pencil, he became eventually a scientific recluse, devoting most of his energy to the solution of obscure mathematical problems. But he was still a magnificent talker; and the Goncourts, at least when Gavarni talked, were always avid listeners, gathering in his stories of the Romantic past, memorizing his sharply original comments upon the manners of the present age.[1] Since there was no question of professional rivalry, admiration and affection could flow unimpeded.

When Gavarni died, they devoted a volume to their old friend's memory. It was one of their happiest critical efforts; and, during the autumn of 1869, Jules was hard at work polishing the last chapters. Both men were frequently indisposed – they suffered from disorders of the nervous system, and from a variety of mysterious ailments centred in the liver and stomach; but hitherto they had been apt to share their maladies and, like identical twins, to suffer equally at the same time. Now Jules's health began to alarm Edmond, although, besides being eight years younger, Jules had been always the gayer of the two, the more energetic and more carefree. To Jules we owe much of the *Journal* from December 2, 1851, when it was launched, until the end of 1869; it was usually Jules who held the pen; and the text itself – lively, mordant, picturesque – up to that point seems to bear the imprint of the younger brother's personality.

Between 1851 and 1869, the dramas that excite them are generally the dramas of their professional life. They are incessantly struggling for fame and recognition, and are constantly defeated, not only by the *bourgeois* philistinism of their age, but by the malice and acrimony of base professional detractors. Simultaneously – and this is the most fascinating aspect of the book – we watch them prosecuting their indefatigable search for 'copy': visiting a hospital to observe a Caesarian section – the patient is a dwarf who has been got with child by a circus-giant: attending a party of fashionable *demi-mondaines* or the cultivated salon of the Princesse Mathilde:

[1] He had paid a long visit to London, where he was well received in literary and fashionable society. 'Gavarni disait de Dickens "qu'il avait une vanité énorme et paralysante peinte sur la figure" '.

persuading a famous courtesan's maid to allow them to explore the secrets of her wardrobe. Flashes of wit allumine the narrative: with obvious satisfaction they produce an elegant phrase to round off the effect of some entertaining anecdote. But now, as 1870 draws on, the atmosphere grows dark and dismal. Jules has entered the region of shadows. One day he makes a characteristic note about the composer Vaucorbeil: *'Quelles sont donc bizarres et singulières.'* he writes, *'les affections universal!'* and proceeds to describe how the unfortunate Vaucorbeil is haunted by a nervous horror of velvet, and how, before he accepts an invitation to dinner, he is obliged to ask his host if the dining-room chairs have velvet coverings. But the next line has been scratched out, and the remainder of the page is crowded with line after line of meaningless dots. Those dots symbolize a breakdown: the pen has fallen from Jules's hand. Henceforward it is taken up by Edmond, whose first task is to chronicle the rapid decline and disintegration of his brother's mental faculties.

He did not flinch from the task that confronted him. If any proof were required of his devotion to his art, of the selfless enthusiasm that inspired a record which contains so many indications of selfishness and pettiness, we may find it in Edmond's heroic perseverance during the period of his greatest misery. Jules expired, fiercely fighting for life, still clutching at the sanity that seemed to escape him hour by hour. Soon he grew suspicious and morose, and even turned against the brother he loved. At other times, he was as timid as a child; and, when they visited a restaurant together and Edmond scolded him for a clumsy movement, he burst into a flood of tears, exclaiming desperately: *'Ce n'est pas de ma faute! Ce n'est pas de ma faute!'* At which, Edmond took his hand, and both wept uncontrollably beneath the eyes of the astonished diners.

From an acquaintance who accompanied the funeral procession, we learn that Edmond's hair became entirely white as he followed Jules's coffin towards the cemetery of Montmartre. It was the supreme drama of his existence, embodied in some of his finest pages. But a second catastrophe was now under way; and Edmond confronted it as coolly and resolutely as he had met the first. If his account of his brother's decline and death is among the most moving works of its kind in nineteenth-century prose literature, his story of the Siege of Paris and the Commune is certainly among the most dramatic. Once again he preserved his *sangfroid*; and again his ability to take notes need not be attributed to any lack of real feeling. He had hated the Commune, since he loathed democracy; but he felt an equal detestation for the ferocious excesses of the Versaillais. His concern is with humanity at large and with the agony of a great city, now plunged into an unearthly silence – '*Je suis frappé, frappé plus que jamais, du silence de mort, que fait un désastre dans une grande ville*' – now shaken by the crash of artillery, as Thiers's troops move in from Versailles and the red-flagged barricades begin to fall. Throughout he maintains the position of an impartial observer, devoting an especially memorable passage to the hardihood displayed by a pair of unknown Communist insurgents. They were standing in the boulevard, just beneath the windows of the apartment where he had taken refuge: '*De l'autre côté du boulevard, il y a étendu à terre un homme, dont je ne vois que les semelles de bottes, et un bout de galon doré. Près du cadavre, se tiennent debout deux hommes: un garde national et un lieutenant. Les balles font pleuvoir sur eux les feuilles d'un petit arbre, qui étend ses branches au-dessus de leurs têtes. Un détail dramatique que j'oubliais. Derrière eux, dans un renfoncement, devant une porte cochère fermée, aplatie tout de son long, et comme rasée sur le trottoir, une femme tient dans une de ses mains un képi – peut-être le képi du tué.*

Le garde national, avec des gestes violents, indignés, parlant à la cantonade, indique aux Versaillais qu'il veut enlever le mort. Des balles continuent à faire pleuvoir des feuilles sur les deux hommes. Alors le garde national, dont j'aperçois la figure rouge de colère, jette son chassepot sur son épaule, la crosse en l'air, et marche sur les coups de fusil, l'injure à la bouche. Soudain, je le vois s'arrêter, porter la main à sa tete, appuyer, une seconde, sa main et son front contre un petit arbre, puis tourner sur lui-même, et tomber sur le dos, le bras en croix.'

Here the typical Goncourt prose style – the celebrated *écriture artiste,* on which they had expended so much pain and thought – is replaced by a simpler, less artificial prose, more in harmony with the character of the crude and terrible events described. None of the occurrences of his later life was to stir Edmond so profoundly; but he lived on until 1896, holding a rather chilly court at his Sunday night gatherings and maintaining a somewhat wary friendship with such intimates as Alphonse Daudet. The desire to observe, and to translate the results of his observation into a permanent literary shape, was still the writer's ruling passion. It was, indeed, almost the only form of activity he had ever understood or valued. He died, as he lived, a remorseless perfectionist, the man of letters above all else; and, although the Goncourts' pursuit of perfection was often inspired by their personal vanity, they set an example worth remembering in our own slovenly and half-hearted age.

George Sand

One cold, wet day in June, 1876, George Sand, otherwise the baronne Dudevant, was buried in the small family cemetery adjoining the gardens of her ancestral country house. To the surprise of some of the mourners, the ceremony was Catholic. But Renan, who attended together with Flaubert, Dumas *fils*, Jérome Bonaparte and Paul Meurice, representing Victor Hugo, thought that the decision had been wise and right; for the cemetery was crowded with peasant women; and *'il ne fallait pas troubler les idées des simples femmes qui venaient prier pour elle, encapuchonnées, avec leur chapelet à la main.'* Later, writing to Turgenev, Flaubert voiced his sense of loss: *'La mort de la pauvre mère Sand m'a fait une peine infinie. J'ai pleuré à son enterrement comme un veau.... Pauvre chère grande femme! ... Il fallait la connaître, comme je l'ai connue, pour savoir tout ce qu'il y avait de féminin dans ce grand homme, l'immensité de tendresse qui se trouvait dans ce génie....'*

It is stimulating to compare the tribute of Flaubert with the ferocious attack once delivered by Baudelaire in his private notebooks. For him, George Sand summed up everything he found contemptible and reprehensible in nineteenth-century literature. He had never encountered her face to face; but were he to do so, he declared, nothing could have prevented him from hurling a holy-water stoup at the wretched woman's head!

La femme Sand est le Prudhomme de l'immoralité.... Elle est bête, elle est lourde, elle est bavarde; elle a, dans les idées morales, la même profondeur de jugement et la même délicatesse de sentiment que les concierges et les filles entretenues. ... Je ne puis penser à cette stupide créature sans un certain frémissement d'horreur.

That Flaubert, who detested his age, and Baudelaire, a no less envenomed critic of the vulgarity of the modern world, should have approached the character and achievement of George Sand from two such entirely different standpoints, is some indication both of the complexity of her career, and of the extent and variety of the ground it covered. Other important witnesses are Balzac, a platonic admirer, and Sainte-Beuve, an old but treacherous friend. Sainte-Beuve's early affection turned, as the years went by, to mistrust and malice; he could see only the more ridiculous aspect of her amatory adventures and intellectual escapades, and dubbed her unfeelingly *'une Christine de Suède à l'estaminet'*.

Balzac, however, was always proud of this extraordinary personage's friendship; and in February 1838 he wrote to Madame Hanska describing at length his first impressions of Nohant. Here was a woman, he felt, of heroic stature – not physically attractive, it was true, but possessed of a vigour and dignity of mind that raised her to his own level. Side by side, they had sat down to converse, his hostess, with her huge brilliant eyes, her dusky olive complexion and recently acquired double chin, wearing a dressing gown, red trousers and yellow embroidered slippers, and had talked for three hours on questions of absorbing interest: *'Je causais avec un camarade. ... Nous avons discuté avec un sérieux, une bonne foi, une candeur, une conscience dignes des grands bergers qui mènent les troupeaux d'hommes, les grandes questions du mariage et de la liberté. ...'*

Balzac added that, by vocation at least, George Sand was not an artist – *'elle ... n'est artiste qu'à l'extérieur'*; and the modern reader who wishes to pick his way among these divergent testimonies must agree that the novelist's genius did not find its full expression, nor could ever have been completely satisfied, in the painstaking creation of works of art. She lacked the fiercely self-critical devotion of a Flaubert or a Baudelaire; her capacity for passionate enthusiasm was accompanied by a considerable strain of insensitiveness and carelessness; and, though she felt strongly on a multitude of problems, she seldom thought originally. Her intelligence was as diffuse as its operations were vigorous. Often the energy she displayed alarmed, as much as it dazzled, her lovers and admirers.

'*Je ne suis pas né comme toi,*' wrote Jules Sandeau plaintively,' *avec un petit ressort d'acier dans le cerveau, dont il ne faut que pousser le bouton pour que la volonté fonctionne....*' At the stormiest moments of a tempestuous existence, she was still capable of producing her nightly ration of twenty sheets of copy, rarely pausing to correct a sentence but covering page after page '*de sa grande écriture tranquille*'. For the cult of perfection as practised by Flaubert – the view of art, as a means not of expressing passion, but of absorbing and transcending it – from her wild youth to her peaceful old age she displayed the utmost disregard.

Thus, the effect she produced on her contemporaries is at least as significant as the novels that she left behind; and her legend and her life-work are now impossible to disentangle. If her character was exceedingly complex, much of that complexity, André Maurois suggested, may be attributed to her ancestral background. Through her mother, she was of proletarian descent; through her father's family, she came of aristocratic and royal stock. Was she not descended from Maurice de Saxe? The Maréchal de Saxe, himself a bastard, had begotten an illegitimate daughter, Marie-Aurore, who, by her second marriage with the cultured financier, Dupin de Francueil, became the grandmother of George Sand. '... *Par sa naissance, placée sur la frontière de deux classes,*' wrote her biographer, '*et, par son éducation, sur une frange où se recontraient le rationalisme du XVIIIe siècle et le romantisme du XIXe*', she blended the libertinism of one age with the romantic idealism of another, and combined a tendency to extravagance and daring with a useful admixture of solid peasant shrewdness. Her tutor, Deschartes, a relic of the eighteenth century, initiated her into masculine pursuits and encouraged her to wear masculine dress. Under his direction she studied anatomy and surgery, learned to shoot and ride in the fields round Nohant, and adopted an attitude of male *camaraderie* towards the young men of the neighbouring town. It was a wholly exceptional *jeune fille* who gave her hand in marriage to that good-natured squireling, Casimir Dudevant, on 10 September 1822.

Already she had learned to prize her freedom – '*ma profession est la liberté*,' she afterwards declared; and freedom and marriage were soon found incompatible. The baron Dudevant finally relinquished his precarious hold upon his wife. But what to do with her freedom, once it had been gained, was a problem that continued to preoccupy her until she was an ageing woman. Should she dominate or must she submit? One side of her temperament was constantly demanding that she should select a worthy master; and she was as regularly disappointed in the masters whom she endeavoured to obey. '*Si Prosper Merimée*,' she observed, '*m'avait comprise, il m'eût peut-être aimée; et s'il m'eût aimée, il m'eût soumise; et si j'avais pu me soumettre à un homme, je serais sauvée, car la liberté me ronge et me tue....*'

The last assertion, however, was not entirely accurate; for just as strong as the inclination to submit was the desire to govern; and, throughout the long series of passionate relationships that engrossed so large a share of the writer's time and energy, she was perpetually vacillating between the masculine and the feminine rôle, and discovering in neither rôle the complete satisfaction after which she hungered. The first version of her novel *Lélia*, contains the portrait of an unsatisfied woman; it seems clear that none of her relationships gave her everything she hoped and dreamed, and that she remained a feminine Don Juan, feverishly pursuing an ideal bliss that somehow still eluded her.

The story of the pursuit is long and intricate; for it was by making love, as much as by writing, that she established emotional and intellectual contact with the world around her. Every new liaison was to be the crown of her life. But, although she was always passionately in earnest, a certain colouring of hypocrisy cannot sometimes be discounted. It was once observed of her romantic novels that, when a heroine wished to change her lover or to discard her husband, the Almighty was generally hovering near to sanctify her change of purpose; and the novelist's wildest caprices were usually indulged with the very highest aims in view. On adultery she endeavoured to confer the sober bloom of domesticity; and, with results that were frequently absurd, she strove to reproduce in each new love the semblance of a genuine conjugal tie. `

A relationship must mean all or nothing; and she despised the chilly comfort offered by Sainte-Beuve, who, after her rupture with Sandeau, wrote recommending *'ces demi-guérisons, ces demi-bonheurs qui, après certaines épreuves, sont encore une assez belle part pour le coeur....'* Jules Sandeau was the first young man whom she dominated in her rôle of motherly mistress, while loudly complaining that he had failed to dominate her; and he was presently followed by Alfred de Musset, the fragile yet demonic dandy, whom she apostrophized in a famous love letter that, were the reader ignorant of the context, he would probably assume to have been addressed by an infatuated man to a very much younger girl. Their association and Musset's subsequent revolt precipitated one of the noisiest literary scandals of the nineteenth century: and, although her attachment to Chopin lasted longer and was severed with considerably less disturbance, in that relationship, too, she played the dominant rôle, and surrounded *'le petit Chopin'* with an intense maternal solicitude that overlaid, and threatened to obliterate him, like a gigantic featherbed.

Such was Sand the *'infirmière passionnée'*, whose masculine strength would appear to have flourished on her lovers' hidden weakness. But, coexistent in the character of the woman whom Alfred d'Orsay was to acclaim as *'le premier homme de notre temps'*, we also distinguish the features of the feminine devotee, restlessly searching for her ideal guardian. Her gratitude, when she believed that she had discovered him, was deep, if often short-lived; and at least as illuminating as the affairs with Chopin and Musset was the liaison that bound her to Michel de Bourges, a provincial tribune of the people, plain and small and prematurely aged – his immense, bald, grotesquely shaped skull wrapped winter and summer in three enormous coloured handkerchiefs – yet armed with a fiery eloquence that carried all before it.

Bourges was a violent Republican; and for a while his mistress became a forthright exponent of modern revolutionary principles, which she continued to support until the dawn of the Second Empire. Simultaneously, she became enamoured of the ideas, but not of the person, of that vacuous reformer, Pierre Leroux, the author of a homemade philosophy that seemed to promise her the Master Word. Much to the alarm of her hard-headed publisher, Buloz – '*Ecrivez à George*,' he implored Sainte-Beuve '*qu'elle ne fasse pas trop de mystique*' – she wandered on to dangerous ground. '*Leroux*,' writes M. Maurois, '*fut le Godwin de ce Shelley femme*.' She sought his advice, supplied him with money, and dragged him across the threshold of several literary drawing rooms. '*Elle l'a poussé*,' Béranger remarked, '*à pondre une petite religion pour avoir le plaisir de la couver*.' But Bourges was an amorous double dealer; and Leroux's little religion eventually proved to be a china egg.

Just as much of her writing was slipshod, so many of her attempts to find a worthy master and to hammer out a private creed – '*la recherche ardente ou mélancolique, mais assidue, des rapports qui peuvent, qui doivent exister entre l'âme individuelle et . . . Dieu*' – lost their way in a fog of romantic wishful thinking. Baudelaire abominated her specious optimism; and it is indeed true that, with the passage of years, her system of beliefs grew vaguer and more loosely framed. The atheist, the scientist, the spiritualist, the orthodox believer were each of them accorded a separate hearing; every critical distinction tended gradually to dissolve and vanish. Flaubert and Balzac, on the other hand, saw that her finest qualities had a very different origin. They depended not on her commerce with ideas, but on her countrywoman's knowledge and love of the rich Berrichon landscape in which she had been brought up. For nearly seventy years, Nohant was the background of her life; and there she died in 1876. Her love of her old house and of the country surrounding it was almost the only love that never failed her.

Houses that have witnessed dramatic events are apt to assume a somewhat haunted air. Not so the Château de Nohant, which looks as placid as a sunny autumn day. It is a plain, nicely proportioned building, its symmetry a little spoiled by the large dormer window of an attic studio, which the novelist, an indulgent mother, constructed for her only son Maurice. You enter from an elm-shaded village square; and opposite the pavilioned gateway stands a humble village church, so diminutive and irregularly shaped and buttressed that it might have been chopped out by a giant spade. But the entrance hall of the château has a modest architectural splendour, with its prettily rainbow-marbled walls and broad circular, iron-railed staircase.

Everything in the house is solid but good – some inlaid cabinets, straight-backed eighteenth-century chairs, boatlike beds under printed cotton hangings and a huge oval table said to have been constructed by the village carpenter. At that table the novelist spent her evenings; and around her sat her favoured guests. What guests she welcomed to Nohant! Chopin, fragile and hollow-eyed, affectionately nicknamed *Chip, Chipette, Chopinsky*; Franz Liszt, who brought Marie d'Agoult, his romantic, ill-used mistress; Delacroix, who, during his stay at the château, painted a famous *Coronation of the Virgin;* Turgenev and the singer Pauline Viardot; Balzac, Théophile Gautier and Gustave Flaubert. Until midnight, the company talked, read or played dominoes; while the novelist herself, if she were not dressmaking or embroidering, very often laid out a game of patience. Then she rose and ascended to her workroom, where she remained for six or seven hours, smoking cigarettes and extinguishing the butts by tossing them away into a glass of water.

Throughout her life she had both an immense capacity for work and an enormous appetite for sober domestic pleasures. Innumerable fêtes were held at Nohant; and about 1848 Maurice Sand, who passed most of his time in attendance on his mother, began to organize a troup of marionettes. He carved their faces and limbs from fine-grained pearwood; and the novelist and her women friends cut and stitched the dresses. Nohant is the museum of a lifetime; you can examine the family portraits with which George Sand decorated her walls – her celebrated ancestor Maurice Saxe, and his love-child, the impetuous Aurore de Saxe; the pianos on which Liszt and Chopin played; her metal bath and her splendidly appointed kitchen, with rows of polished copper pots; even the fossils she collected and the pressed flowers that she enjoyed preparing; her blue silk hat, her fan, her walking stick and her capacious leather bag. But most stirring of all are the marionette theatre and Maurice's puppets in their dusky cases – big puppets some eighteen inches high, suspended in their glass-walled prison like souls in purgatory who await deliverance.

We know their names – Balandard, the director of the cast; the comtesse de Bombrecoulant, a voluptuous lady of fashion; Colonel Vertébral, a hard-bitten military man; Bassinet, the gamekeeper; and Bamboula, a seductive coloured girl. But who is the fascinating female centaur – a Bardot of the centaur world – with her dappled equine hide, her coroneted golden hair and swelling breasts? And what has become of the many plays they performed? On the walls of the marionette theatre, which at Nohant occupied the place of a former billiard room, and contained both a puppet stage and an elaborate stage for human actors, hangs a carefully printed playbill, announcing the first presentation, 'with dogs and sound effects,' of a one act drama entitled *La Chambre Bleue*, on Saturday 28 April 1863. An audience of fifty often occupied the theatre; and they were encouraged

42

to make their own interventions and themselves address the actors; at which the actors always answered back.

Meanwhile, little by little, she had discovered that she was growing old. Yet hers, she noted, was an astonishing old age – '*cette étonnante vieillesse qui s'est faite pour moi sans infirmité et sans lassitude.*' Never a regularly attractive woman – she was too sallow and too sharp-featured: the brother of her Venetian gallant, Pagello, referred to her disparagingly as '*cette sardine*' – she had soon forfeited her youthful slimness. In 1864, when she was sixty, she met her husband for the last time. To the rest of the world she was the famous Madame George Sand; but Casimir Dudevant, living in the past, preferred to employ her baptismal name of Aurore. At that last meeting, however, it seemed oddly inapplicable. She had ceased, he murmured sadly, to suggest the youthful Dawn Goddess: '*elle ressemblait plutôt à un soleil couchant.*' Yes, her figure was plump: her cheeks were drooping and heavy. But the setting sun had another twelve years in which to shed its broad declining beams; and those years formed a period of incessant activity and of much spontaneous, unforced gaiety.

She loved the country as passionately as ever, still carried off her guests to swim the deep pools of the river Indre. Her daughter, the exquisite Solange, had escaped from a stormy marriage with the sculptor Clésinger, and now roamed the cities of Europe with various vague protectors. But Maurice was a devoted son; and all the novelist's affection went out to her young and charming grandchildren. She had acquired, without effort or self-consciousness, the difficult art of 'being a grandmother'. Besides cutting and sewing the children's frocks, she instructed them in reading, history, geography and the mysteries of French prose. Little Aurore, in whom she glimpsed perhaps a replica of herself, was an especial favourite. 'She understands too quickly . . . understanding fascinates her: having to learn discourages her.' She enjoyed the liveliness they had brought to Nohant: '*Mon Dieu, que la vie est bonne quand tout ce qu'on aime est vivant et grouillant!*'

Few passionate and headstrong women have accepted old age so calmly and so gracefully. Now an authoritative yet devotedly affectionate matriach, she had retained her power of loving and suffering. But pretentious ideologies had ceased to attract her; she fell back on a painfully acquired fund of sober pagan wisdom. *'La tristesse n'est pas malsaine'* she had written to Flaubert eleven years before her death, *'elle nous empêche de nous dessécher.'* And, a year later, to Charles Poncy, in November 1866: *'On est heureux par soi-même quand on sait s'y prendre: avoir des goûts simples, un certain courage, une certaine abnégation. . . . Donc, le bonheur n'est pas une chimère, j'en suis sûre à present; moyennant l'expérience et la réflexion, on tire de soi beaucoup . . . Vivons donc la vie comme elle est, sans ingratitude.'*

Ego Hugo

'Genius' is one of those mysterious and magical words which are more stimulating than enlightening. Nobody can explain to us just what genius is; and the critic who pretends to recognize it in a member of his own generation almost always proves to have been grotesquely misguided. Yet, now and then, an artist emerges who, even during his youth, commands general respect and awe – Victor Hugo, for example, a poet who seems to have differed from the rest of mankind, not only in his splendid literary gifts (which enabled him to compose a long series of best-selling masterpieces) but in the chemical composition of his nerves and sinews.

He had tremendous physical vitality, prodigious mental energy. His outward appearance was impressive – Hugo resembled a lion, though admittedly a rather small lion. He had, moreover, remarkable strength of will, not always to be distinguished from an iron-clad selfishness. At the age of seventy-two, he suffered his first attack of toothache, and found the experience strangely puzzling. When he had passed the age of eighty, he continued, in the bitterest winter weather, to walk the streets without a greatcoat, observing in his large, grand way that his 'youth', he had discovered, was all the coat he needed. At the same period of his existence, he would climb unaided onto the roof of a Parisian omnibus; and the omnibus frequently carried him towards a secret rendezvous. At every age, he had been a passionate lover of women; and, within a few months of his death, Hugo's amatory behaviour still resembled that of King David.

Most creative careers have their ups and downs – bursts of

45

fierce activity are followed by long dull intervals of lassitude and melancholy; after many years of popular applause, the artist's supporters may fall away and his warmest admirers begin to shake their heads. No such unhappy reverses chequered the career of Victor Hugo. Triumph succeeded triumph. But, if there was one triumphal moment more conspicuous than the others, it occurred in 1830, when his poetic tragedy, *Hernani*, a boldly unconventional piece of work, was presented for the first time on the stage of the Comédie Française, amid scenes that resembled the sudden outbreak of a civil war.

Since conservative critics were determined to damn the play, Victor Hugo had marshalled his own troop of intellectual men-at-arms. Prominent among them was Théophile Gautier, distinguished by his rose-red medieval doublet, his light-sea-green trousers and his velvet-collared coat. Many lines were greeted with roars of derision: Hugo's defenders roared back. Words were accompanied by blows; skirmishes were fought all over the theatre; but the aggressive demeanour of the Romantic shock troops ensured that *Hernani* obtained at least a partial hearing. More beautiful than ever, though pale with exhaustion, Madame Victor Hugo presided over her husband's victory. He was swept home again on a flood of enthusiasm, distributing solemn handshakes and congratulating his weary lieutenants on the noble service they had rendered. '*Gérard, je suis content de vous*', he informed a particularly courageous young man; and the future author of *Sylvie* felt that he had been amply repaid.

The Battle of *Hernani*, however, was not only one of the greatest occasions in the career of Victor Hugo: it also marked the apogee of the French Romantic movement. That movement had had a pervasive effect. Besides colouring the outlook of writers and painters, and exercising a profound influence in the sphere of personal life, it had left its trace on the fashions of the day, which faithfully reflected the prevailing mode of sentiment. It inspired dress designers as well as poets; and among the arbiters of fashion in the eighteen-hirties was the brilliant draughtsman, Sulpice-Guillaume

Chevalier, who worked under the name Gavarni. Twenty-six at the time of the famous Battle, he was a regular contributor to the pages of *La Mode* and, in 1833, founded his own fashion paper which he called *Le Journal des Gens du Monde*. For the latter publication, Gavarni both invented the fashions and supplied the fashion plates. An expert lithographer, he drew direct on the stone; and detached specimens of his exquisitely diaphanous designs can still be discovered – or could be discovered a few years ago – in the bookshops of the Left Bank. The dresses he had imagined, and the women who wear them, seem as light as butterflies. This was a period, Gérard de Nerval remembered – the same Gérard who had received Hugo's resounding commendation for services rendered at the Comédie Française – when passions were pure but intense, hopes were exalted and yet vague. And, while the dandies, of whom Gavarni was one, modelled themselves on Beau Brummell, with certain suggestions of Lord Byron, their feminine counterparts aspired to an air of 'ideal seraphicity'. The type of the ethereal consumptive – presently to be immortalized by Dumas *fils* in the heroine of *La Dame aux Camélias* – had originated during the eighteen-thirties. Distinction tended to droop; beauty must expect an early death.

Thus the fashions that Gavarni created are designed to produce an impression of fragility and volatility, as if the wearers had just descended to earth or were just on the point of taking flight. Huge wing-like sleeves spring from their shoulders; tightly pinched waists accentuate the breadth of their skirts, which are lifted an inch or two above the ground, disclosing narrow flat-soled shoes, often secured round the ankles with crossed ribbons. The stuffs employed were appropriately fine in texture – 'unbleached batiste, watered muslin, checked barege, and embroidered organdie muslin'. But, whereas even ball dresses were simple and inexpensive, the jewellery that went with them was costly and elaborate. We read, for instance, at a slightly earlier period, how Madame Gross-Davillier appeared at a ball in Paris, wearing diamonds of inestimable value with a dress that had cost only thirty-five *louis d'or* and twenty francs' worth of flowers. The Romantic spirit has always favoured extremes and delighted in the use of contrasts.

When they remembered the pleasures of the thirties, writers and artists, who survived into the heyday of the Second Empire, felt that they were looking back across the landscape of a lost world. Sentiment had been replaced by sensuality, ethereal elegance by vulgar luxury. Hugo himself may perhaps have regretted the past; for, although no period came altogether amiss to him, and he would have played a prominent role upon any stage, the thirties were the epoch of his youth, when genius and innocence had walked hand in hand. Not long after the production of *Hernani*, he had learned that his beautiful and apparently devoted wife was at length growing a little tired of her Olympian privileges. She preferred to live on a less exacting level; and into Adèle's confidence had crept one of her husband's closest friends, Charles-Augustin de Sainte-Beuve, a man as diffident, depressed and self-conscious as the celebrated poet whom she had married – and whose signet-ring bore the magniloquent legend *Ego Hugo* – was passionate and self-assured. Sainte-Beuve had a sensitiveness, a feminine delicacy, that Victor Hugo altogether lacked.

Confronted with the discovery that he was in danger of losing his wife, the poet vociferated like an injured Titan. But Adèle continued to meet Sainte-Beuve; and, although the union of Adèle and Victor Hugo never completely broke down – she managed his houshold, cared for his children and helped him entertain his friends – she resigned the part of muse and mistress to an attractive young player named Juliette Drouet. Many one-time devoted husbands, finding sympathy and affection denied them at home, have looked for consolation abroad. But only Hugo could have organized his new love affair with such magisterial egotism. If Adèle had been his impatient helper, Juliette Drouet was to become his abject slave. Her servitude lasted for fifty years; and in the whole history of human relationships there are few more surprising or more pathetic episodes. When

Juliette first encountered Hugo during the spring of 1832, she was a somewhat unruly young woman of twenty-six, better known for her beauty than for her talents as a serious actress. She had already borne a child to the sculptor Pradier; and recently she had lived under the protection of Prince Anatole Demidoff, an extravagant and dissipated Russian millionaire. Hugo demanded – and his demand was immediately granted – not only that Juliette should say goodbye to her past, but that for the remainder of her existence she should lead the life of a penitent nun. With profound humility, she accepted her lot. Demidoff's sumptuous gifts were thrown aside; her theatrical career was at length abandoned. She retired to small and modest rooms, from which she was seldom allowed to emerge save under proper chaperonage. She submitted an exact account of her daily expenses, which the poet – never a Romantic in questions of money – always carefully and sternly looked through.

For these sacrifices, what was Juliette's reward? The consciousness that Hugo loved her, although, as time went by, he grew habitually and extensively unfaithful. Permission to follow him wherever he went, provided she kept at a modest distance – to the Channel Islands, after he had refused to support the usurpation of Napoleon III, and back again in 1870 amid the acclamations of Republican Paris. Last of all – since they were often separated, even while she and the master of her destiny inhabited the same neighbourhood – the opportunity of writing him one-thousand-and-one love letters. To the end, she remained intensely jealous. But, such was the domination that her lover exercised, such her unquestioning acceptance of Hugo's view of himself as one of those spirits who have been born to mould a century, that the idea of rebellion seems scarcely to have crossed her mind.

Juliette died in 1883; and Hugo survived her for another two years, a sturdy white-bearded patriarch, with rosy cheeks and piercing eyes. Undismayed, he observed the approach of death. Victor Hugo and his Creator had always been on good terms; and, when he addressed God as he was often inclined to do – for, although not an orthodox Christian, he worshipped a Supreme Being – it was as if an independent prince were writing to a friendly emperor. Like himself, God could afford to be careless. The divine artist too (he had noted in a sonorous poem) was occasionally guilty of bad taste, creating now an exquisite humming-bird, now a hideous behemoth, and weaving beauty and deformity into the pattern of the same fabric. Before long, he and his creator would meet; and this was a prospect that uplifted and delighted him. 'I am old, I am going to die (he exclaimed to a young poetess). I shall see God face to face. See God! Speak to Him! A great occasion indeed! But what shall I say? I often think of it. I am preparing my speech. . . .'

On 22 May 1885, the news went out tnat Victor Hugo had died. Both the senate and the Chamber suspended their sittings as a tribute to the dead man; and, on the night of the 31st, two million Frenchmen accompanied his coffin through the torch-lit streets of Paris. Overhead gigantic scutcheons bore the names of his most famous books: *Les Misérables*, *Les Feuilles d'Automne*, *Quatre-vingt-treize*. He was buried in the vaults of the Pantheon, a monument to the heroes of his race, constructed on his own scale.

Oscar Wilde

The generation that knew Oscar Wilde, not as a subject of literary legend but as friend, confidant, exemplar, antagonist, victim, has now almost entirely disappeared. Yet in the nineteen-twenties there were still numerous survivors. Ada Leverson, the gifted and kindly woman who sheltered Wilde at her London house during the dreadful period between his two trials when every other door was shut against him, lived on until 1933. Though Robert Ross, after Wilde's release from imprisonment his devoted supporter and long-suffering financial adviser, died in 1918, Reginald Turner, who, together with Ross, had attended the stricken writer's deathbed, remained to tell the tale another two decades.

Then, of course, there was Lord Alfred Douglas, who left the world he had adorned, if not ennobled, as recently as 1945. I remember being taken to visit him at his dismal seaside rooms, where, no longer 'a gilded pillar of infamy' but a grey and shrunken relic of the past, he offered us tea and sugared cakes, and discussed the modest bets that he was fond of placing through a local bookie, yet continued to exhibit, despite his age and decrepitude, some of the lackadaisical airs and graces of an attractive, brilliant, spoiled young man.

On one point all Wilde's former friends with whom I have spoken seemed to be unanimously agreed. Wilde was an extraordinarily good-natured and warm-hearted person: there was nothing harsh or tyrannical about his wit. Mrs Leverson described his spontaneous charm; and the popular novelist, Mrs Belloc Lowndes, who had known him far less well, described a dinner party at 16 Tite Street, when Mr and Mrs Oscar Wilde had entertained the local clergyman and his shy and homely wife, and related how Wilde had gone to immense pains to raise this tedious lady's spirits, talking to her of shipwrecks (which she confessed she dreaded) and explaining in elaborate and fantastic detail the precautions he himself employed. He always travelled, he said, with his private hencoop, on which, if the vessel should sink, he proposed to float away across the ocean.

Wilde, I am assured, never directed his satirical shafts against the obscure and unassuming. He radiated light, good-humoured fun; and, although in his later years he became a trifle coarse and flabby, during his happiest days he produced the general impression of being uncommonly large but reassuringly robust. As for his talk, there was no describing it. None of his admirers could quite do justice to the effect; they declared that the qualities he revealed in his books were but a shadow of his conversational powers. He wrote divertingly; he talked inimitably, mixing nonsense, paradox and bravado with rare flights of poetic imagination. As he informed André Gide, he had put his talents into his writing; into his life went all his real genius.

He had planned his existence as a perfect work of art; and within a few weeks, during the spring of 1895, that vision was conclusively and brutally shattered. The good-hearted dandy had become involved in a conflict between two malevolent human beings whose allied characters were exactly the opposite of his own – 'Bosie' Douglas, the golden youth he adored, and Bosie's hated father, the ferocious 'Scarlet Marquess,' both personages in whom hatred and revenge burned even more strongly than their other violent passions. Wilde succumbed; the dandy's masterpiece was ruined. For the five years of life that remained to him, Oscar Wilde was a seedy, impoverished exile. The story has a tragic completeness; hence its hold on the minds of modern readers. Did Wilde himself fully grasp its pattern? He had confided to André Gide, on the eve of his downfall, that he was momentarily expecting some catastrophe; and he seems to have guessed that he had already committed the fatal act of hubris.

As we study his letters, we watch the tragic process gradually materializing. We see the ambitious, self-confident youth, who had early learned the gift of showmanship and had startled American lecture audiences by appearing on the platform with long, dishevelled ambrosial locks, his massive frame clad in a velvet coat, knee-breeches and silk stockings, develop into the successful dramatist whose virtuosity dominated the London stage. Meanwhile, he had married and begotten two sons; and his married life, on the surface at least – Mrs Wilde is reported to have been an earnest, innocent, unsuspicious woman – was both happy and respectable.

Then alarming notes begin to creep in: his vocabulary becomes more and more florid, his affection for personable young men more and more demonstrative. As early as 1888, the year that witnessed the birth of his second son, he tells a youthful protégé that he himself 'would sacrifice anything for a new experience', and that 'there is an unknown land full of strange flowers and subtle perfumes ... a land where all things are perfect and poisonous.' Finally, in 1891, he meets Lord Alfred Douglas, then only twenty-one years old, a poet whose 'slim gilt soul' (Wilde assured him) oscillated between poetry and passion, a 'wilful, fascinating, irritating, destructive, delightful personality,' at the same time an experienced pederast, thoroughly conversant with all the ways of the homosexual underworld. The older man could never resist his spell, though afterwards he learned to hate him. 'Boys, brandy and betting monopolize his soul,' Wilde concluded bitterly in 1900.

Homosexuality was not so much the direct cause of Oscar Wilde's downfall as the means by which, through the other defects of his character – his vanity, levity and self-indulgent sloth – that downfall was at length accomplished. Having claimed that his previous existence was a work of art, he endeavoured, in the long letter he wrote Alfred Douglas from Reading Gaol, to pretend that his misfortunes had lent him a tragic dignity, and that the work of art was still more impressive because its finale had been dark and terrible. As his letters show, the hope was unfulfilled; Wilde's heroic resolutions very soon evaporated. Instead of the life of chastity, seclusion and hard work, to which he had thought that he aspired in prison, he accepted an existence of fugitive pleasures, idleness, irrealizable dreams, desultory tippling and random sponging.

Yet the later letters, those written between May 1897, when he left prison, and November 1900, when he died at a shabby Parisian hotel, are among the pleasantest that have been collected. He was shifty and feckless, and he nagged his friends for money; but the old inimitable Oscar was not yet extinct. And, once he had abandoned every effort at decorum and stood forth frankly in his true shape – 'there is no such thing as changing one's life: one merely wanders round and round within the circle of one's own personality'; and elsewhere: 'How evil it is to buy Love! ... And yet what purple hours one can snatch from that grey slowing-moving thing we call time!' – he re-emerges as the gayest and wittiest of epistolary scribblers. He still has faithful allies, whose patience and fortitude he often tries; but his favourite companions are the 'little friends' whom he encounters in cafés and along the boulevards. 'Henri plies up and down all day, and has the sweetest and most compromising smiles for me, especially when I am with friends.' Armando is an 'elegant young Roman Sporus ... but his requests for raiment and neckties were incessant: he really bayed for boots, as a dog moonwards.' 'A slim brown Egyptian, rather like a handsome bamboo walking stick, occasionally serves me drinks at the Café d'Egypte.'

'The Ballad of Reading Gaol' was the last attempt Wilde made to reaffirm his literary character; but it had not, he felt, been very fortunate. 'I think bits of the poem very good now, but I will never again out-Kipling Henley.' Although he often struggled to begin a new play, he understood that it was an almost hopeless effort; 'As regards a comedy ... I have lost the mainspring of life and art, *la joie de vivre*.' He had still 'pleasures and passions,' he explained, 'but the joy of life is gone.' Gone, too, was the stimulus of vanity – 'in the old days half of my strength'. During his imprisonment, Wilde had professed to believe that 'nothing really at any period of my life was ever of the smallest importance to me compared with art.' In fact, his art had always been the servant of his personal ambition and his personal desires. He retained, however, the imaginative insight that, once he had ceased to over-dramatize it, helped him to understand his own nemesis: 'I was a problem for which there was no solution.' He had been 'deeply affected,' he wrote after visiting his wife's grave, 'with a sense also of the uselessness of all regret. Nothing could have been otherwise, and Life is a very terrible thing.'

Although he could be solemn on the subject of his literary record, he knew that his finest achievement had been the least serious – *The Importance of Being Earnest*, an elegant piece of nonsense in the mood of Congreve, 'written by a butterfly for butterflies.' The amiable butterfly, alas, fell into the clutches of a system that punished and humiliated without reforming. The punishment continued so long as he lived. 'What astonishes and interests me about my present position,' he wrote on 25 November 1897, 'is that the moment the world's forces begin to persecute anyone they *never leave off*.'

André Gide

'I have a kind of strange feeling,' confided Boswell to a private notebook, 'as if I wished nothing to be secret that concerns myself.' Wrapped in a magnificent 'great coat of Green Camlet lined with Foxskin fur,' holding under his arm a 'hat with sollid gold lace, at least, with the air of being sollid,' he had bounced across the threshold of Jean-Jacques Rousseau's modest hermitage several years earlier; but he had not then studied the *Confessions*, which were withheld from the public till 1781; and the two great masters of autobiographical writing would seem to have reached the same conclusion by entirely separate paths.

Boswell's autobiography, composed of numerous letters, diaries and brilliant fragmentary personal sketches, has not yet been fully published; and it was the *Confessions* that influenced the nineteenth century and encouraged writer after writer to endeavour to lay bare his inmost heart. Baudelaire failed to complete *Mon Coeur Mis à Nu*, the terrible volume that, had it ever been published, would, so he informed his mother, have roused against him the whole human race; but we still have literary surgeons sharpening their knives to probe the maladies of their own souls. It is only nineteen years ago that André Gide laid down his scalpel.

The last operation that Gide performed was among the deepest and the cruellest. *Et Nunc Manet in Te, suivi de Journal Intime*, of which a private edition limited to thirteen copies came out in 1947, is a discursion on his married life, followed by certain extracts, previously suppressed, from his private journal. Gide shared Boswell's hankering to leave nothing that concerned himself behind a veil of 'good taste'; and, having been at work on a self-portrait since he first took pen in hand, he evidently decided, at the close of his career, that some details of his personal conduct had not been thoroughly exhibited. It was a characteristic decision, revealing the odd mixture of sensitiveness and ruthlessness – both carried to remarkable extremes – that seems to have distinguished him throughout his long existence.

A 'man of feeling' in the eighteenth-century style, he combined the exquisite, at times mawkish, sensibility of a Jean-Jacques Rousseau with the clinical curiosity of a modern scientist: and though *Et Nunc Manet in Te* has a disconcerting and repulsive side – he is almost painfully in earnest, positively lachrymose in his determination to hold nothing back and abandon every comforting reticence – it is ennobled by the dispassionate skill with which he rends the veil apart. Already he had told us much. In *L'Immoraliste* and *Si le grain ne meurt* he had portrayed some agonizing stages in the lengthy process of self-discovery, and had explained how his inborn puritanism came into conflict with passions that he could neither suppress nor excuse; how he confronted the manifold problems raised by his homosexual temperament. Amid sensual adventures he was still the puritan; but he could never accept the puritan code, or subscribe to a conviction that the pleasures he pursued were necessarily worthless and degrading. The Immoralist did not lose his way; he discovered what for him was the inevitable and proper course, though by doing so he destroyed his relationship with the women to whom he had been most indebted.

Marceline, the heroine of *L'Immoraliste*, is calm, unselfish, virtuous, prudent. '*Mais qu'avais-je besoin de tranquille bonheur? Celui que me donnait et que représentait pour moi Marceline, était comme un repos pour qui ne se sent pas fatigué.*' Marceline, one guessed, was drawn from the author's wife; and, in this footnote to his novels, Gide stresses her affinity with the type of woman whom he had so often depicted – the pure-minded sisterly companion, doomed to be made miserable by the restless adventures of the man whom she attempts to save, and who never ceases to admire her purity, though, owing to the tempestuous exigencies of his own nature, he finds he cannot profit by it. Such, apparently, was the secret history of Gide's tormented married life. As a young and comparatively innocent man, he had proposed to his cousin, a charming and attractive girl. He had had doubts; but he was reassured by a doctor, whose medical worldly wisdom proved entirely valueless; and he is at considerable pains to make it clear to the reader that his marriage, from the beginning, involved very little physical contact.

Madeleine aroused devotion: she could not awake desire. Her mother had disgraced the family name; and Madeleine had therefore a scrupulous aversion from any form of irregular conduct. She belonged to the same spotless category as the woman whom hitherto he had known and loved best '... *ma mère d'abord ... Mademoiselle Shackleton ... mes tantes Claire et Lucile, modèles de décence, d'honnêté, de reserve, à qui le prêt du moindre trouble de la chair eût fait injure';* and it did not occur to him to associate her in any sensual reverie. For his sensuality worked through the brain; and, since imagination exalted his wife, he could not envisage any sensual gesture that might have tended to drag her down. Had he been less imaginative, he might have been more compassionate. For, after all, pondered the elderly widower, Madeleine, too, may have had emotions – even passions – that she did not confess, and he had never sought to gratify:

Comme elle me paraissait toute âme et de corps, toute fragilité, je n'estimais pas que ce fût la priver beaucoup, de lui soustraire une partie de moi, que je comptais pour d'autant moins importante que je ne pouvais pas la lui donner. ... Entre nous, jamais une explication ne fut tentée. De sa part, jamais une plainte: rien qu'une résignation muette. ...

Were the book merely a story of discord – between a cold, pious, long-suffering woman and a restless, inquisitive and sensual man – even as related by Gide it would be only moderately absorbing. In fact, it possesses a stronger appeal;

for it describes not a gradual dissociation but a continuous obsession, and shows the spiritual hold exerted by Madeleine over a famous husband of whom she could never bring herself to approve, but whom she never renounced or upbraided. In his life she was the embodiment of conscience – the conscience to which he had been taught to harken during the days of his sheltered Protestant childhood; she represented an aspect of his own character to which he had been repeatedly, deliberately, often rapturously untrue, but which, at the moments of his greatest infidelity, he did not fail to respect and cherish. It was a question not simply of loving his wife, but of being unable to refrain from paying allegiance to the standards that she symbolized. She was a 'part of himself' in the most accurate sense of the phrase; and, when her physical presence was removed, as her emotional support had been removed at a far more distant period, the apostle of pagan self-fulfilment felt broken and deserted and old.

In his apologia – if that is the correct term – Gide tells first of the death of his wife, how he received the news and how the shock affected him: then discusses their hidden relationship, and gives pathetic glimpses of their ill-fated *voyage de noces*. Until he produced *Les Faux Monnayeurs*, every book that he published contained some reflection of Madeleine: *'j'ai tout écrit pour la convaincre, pour l'entrainer. Tout cela n'est qu'un long plaidoyer.'* But, although his books were addressed to her, she did not always cut the pages. If she did, she knew that she would disapprove; moreover, she felt that she had no right to attempt to sway his judgment. Thus she retreated into mute resignation, reinforced by moral obstinacy, living alone at his country house – whither a mysterious spell kept incessantly pulling him back – spending her days in meaningless domestic duties and dismally comfortless good works.

At this point, the novelist arises. I do not mean that the narrative smacks of fiction, but that the vignette-picture of Madeleine at Cuverville is drawn with all the delicacy of a highly practised storyteller:

Sans cesse affairée, elle trottait d'un pas menu d'un bout à l'autre de la maison ou du jardin; on la voyait passer, souriante mais insaisissable, et j' obtenais à grand'peine qu'elle m'accordât une heure pour une lecture souvent interrompue par une des bonnes qui venait lui demander aide ou conseil ...

Gentle, if not indulgent, towards others, she was intolerably harsh towards herself. Every day, in all weathers, she would go out to neighbouring farmyards to feed starving dogs and stray cats:

Elle allait ainsi, tenant gauchement devant elle dans ses mains nues une énorme basine où refroidissait la pâtée qu'elle leur avait préparée. Ses mains offertes à la gelée, à la pluie. ... je les voyais s'abmîmer de jour en jour davantage, devenir toujours plus impropres à tous autres travaux que les plus vulgaires. ...

This obstinate course of self-immolation went on year by year, possibly strengthening rather than weakening, though he constantly protested against the harm she did herself, her obsessive hold upon her husband's mind. Was he still hoping for sympathy, forgiveness, for some understanding that would symbolize the ultimate reconciliation of the two personalities at war within his own nature? But Madeleine declined to give away – *'Rien de bon ne peut sortir de là,'* she used to remark, coldly and succinctly, of any line of behaviour that did not conform to her exacting moral standards; and at length, when both had grown old, she dealt him the final and most dreadful blow.

She burned the whole collection of letters that he had written her since his early youth. *'Elle a fait cela, m'a-t-elle dit, sitôt après mon départ pour l'Angleterre. Oh! je sais bien qu'elle a souffert atrocement de mon départ avec Marc; mais devait-elle se venger sur le passé?'* The results of this symbolic gesture – of this ritual punishment, one might say – were profound and lingering. The victim's grief was beyond all measure; and he expresses it in immoderate terms. Probably the pain she inflicted – Madeleine obviously was not a vindictive woman – went much deeper beneath the surface than she either expected or could have understood; and the lull that followed the storm had never the beauty of real peace. As he stood beside her deathbed, it was her gravity, her look of austere distinction, he noted above all else: *'de sorte ... que le dernier regard que je portais sur elle devait me rappeler, non point son ineffable tendresse, mais le sévère jugement qu'elle avait dû porter sur ma vie.'* Again genius must retire discomfited. Inflexible virtue had had the last word.

The Secret Commonwealth

One evening in the year 1692, the Reverend Robert Kirk, Minister of Aberfoyle in Perthshire, an erudite and inquisitive divine who had published a Gaelic version of the Metrical Psalms and helped to translate the Bible into Irish, happened, on some unknown occasion, to walk in his nightgown across a *Dun-shi*, or fairy mount, just behind his parsonage. Suddenly he swooned away and from that moment, it would appear, never regained consciousness. His wife and neighbours gave him up for dead; but, according to a story related by Scott in his *Demonology and Witchcraft*, 'after the ceremony of a seeming funeral' his incorporeal image visited a member of his family 'and commanded him to go to Grahame of Duchray ... "Say to Duchray, who is my cousin ... that I am not dead but a prisoner in Fairy Land. ..." ' There, as it turned out, the Minister was doomed to remain, since Duchray, whom he had instructed how to procure his release, inexplicably bungled the operation. Yet, although he could not escape from captivity, Kirk did not abandon his clerical career; and he was later reputed to have obtained preferment as Chaplain to the Fairy Court.

Robert Kirk met the fate he deserved – considering his previous researches, he should have known better than to walk across a *Dun-shi*; for among the unpublished works that he left in his study was a manuscript entitled *The Secret Commonwealth, An Essay of the Nature and Actions of the Subterranean (and, for most Part,) Invisible People, heretofoir going under the Name of ELVES, FAUNES, and FAIRIES, or the lyke ... as they are described by those who have the*

SECOND SIGHT; and now to occasion further Inquiry, collected and compared, by a Circumspect Inquirer residing
among the Scottish-Irish in Scotland.

This treatise, did not finally achieve publication until 1815,
when it was printed by James Ballantyne from a copy preserved in the Advocates' Library of Edinburgh. Although dis-
appointingly brief, it is a fascinating and instructive essay;
for here is a learned author at work during the second half
of the seventeenth century, while Natural Science was revealing a new earth and a new heaven, who accepts the
existence of a vast realm of supernatural beings, placed on
the frontiers of the world of men and constantly, if rather
vaguely, involved with the affairs of ordinary human life.

Kirk's description of their economy, moreover, is curious
and unexpected. Compared with the beings he portrays,
Shakespeare's sprites are mere figments of poetic fantasy,
creatures of the dramatist's mind rather than products of his
native soil. Kirk's invisible people are mysterious and elusive;
but they constitute a nation apart and have adopted a definite
social scheme; 'they are distributed in Tribes and Orders, and
have Children, Nurses, Marriages, Deaths and Burialls, in
appearance, even as we (unless they do so for a Mock-show,
or to prognosticate such things among us.)' Particularly
stimulating is the account he provides of their tricky and
perilous relationship with representatives of the human
species.

At this point, the contemporary psychologist might perhaps be interested to take a hand. Baudelaire once said of
the Almighty that, even if God did not exist, it would be
necessary to invent Him; and Kirk's fairies, on a completely
different level, belong to the category of beliefs that, whether
supported or unsupported by evidence, seem to respond to a
deep-felt human need. Incidentally, a belief in the Fairy
Kingdom helps to solve some archaeological problems. Who
but the ancient subterranean race could have reared those
green hillocks – often surprisingly large and evidently constructed by artificial means – that break the smooth outline
of so many British downs and moors? These are the

Places called Fairie-hills, which the Mountain People think impious and dangerous to peel or discover, by taking Earth or Wood from them ... In the nixt Country to that of my former Residence, about the year 1676, when there was some Scarcity of Graine, a marvelous Illapse and Vision strongly struck the Imagination of two Women in one Night, living at a good Distance from one another, about a Treasure hid in a Hill called *Sithbhruaich*, or Fayrie-hill. The Appearance of a Treasure was first represented to the Fancy, and then an audible Voyce named the Place where it was to their Awaking Senses. Whereupon both arose, and meitting accidentallie at the Place, discovered their Designe; and joyntly digging, found a Vessell, as large as a Scottish Peck, full of small Pieces of good Money, of ancient Coyn; which halving betuixt them, they sold in Dish-fulls for Dish-fulls of Meall to the Countrey People. Very many of undoubted Credit saw, and had of the Coyn to this Day. But whither it was a good or bad Angell, one of the subterranean People, or the restless Soul of him who hid it, and to what End it was done, I leave to the Examination of others.

They, too, the inhabitants of the secret commonwealth, are the artificers of these delicate flint arrowheads, often to be picked up among the thyme and scabious of some turfy hillside. Their weapons are

nothing of Iron, but much of Stone, like to soft yellow Flint spa, shaped like a Barbed Arrow-head, but flung like a Dairt, with great Force. These Armes (cut by Airt and Tools it seems beyond humane) have somewhat of the Nature of Thunderbolt subtilty, and mortally wounding the vital Parts without breaking the Skin ; of which Wounds I have observed in Beasts, and felt felt them with my Hands. They are not as infallible Benjamites, hitting at a Hair's-breadth; nor are they wholly unvanquishable.

The subterranean race, in fact, can almost always be vanquished by iron – for cold iron, as Odysseus proved when he descended into the world of the dead, will prevail against the encroachments of every supernatural entity; and it was with swords, forged of iron or steel, that the peasant visionaries, the Men of Second Sight, whom Kirk consulted, had from time to time encountered them. Thus he had frequently spoken to a local seer

who in his Transport told he cut the Bodie of one of those People in two with his Iron Weapon, and so escaped this Onset, yet he saw nothing left behind of that appearing Divyded; at other times he wrestled some of them. His Neibours often perceaved this Man to disappear at a certain Place, and about one Hour after to become visible. . . . It was in that Place where he became invisible, said he, that the Subterraneans did encounter and combate with him.

When a man was struck with an elf-shot, his health and energy would gradually decline. Such victims are 'called FEY'; and the injury they have sustained

makes them do somewhat verie unlike their former Practice, causing a sudden Alteration, yet the Cause thereof unperceaveable at present. . . . The Cure of such Hurts is, only for a Man to find out the Hole with his Finger; as if the Spirits flowing from a Man's warme Hand were Antidote sufficient against their poyson's Dairts.

The subterranean people, indeed, are responsible for many of the symptoms of psychosomatic maladies; and Kirk's belief in their existence would seem to have been strengthened by his observations of that extraordinary phenomenon of mental derangement which German authorities call the *doppelganger*[1].

This type of hallucination – either an exact reflection of the person who beholds it, or an image of himself endowed with a sinister independent life – has been described by writers as different as Goethe, Alfred de Musset, Maupassant, Dostoievski and Rudyard Kipling. Kirk had decided that this 'Reflex-man' or 'Co-Walker, every way like the Man, as a Twin-brother and Companion, haunting him as his Shadow', was but another example of subterranean mischief. The shadow that follows the man, and may also precede him, 'is often seen and known among Men . . . both before and after the Originall is dead'. But death eventually severs the link;

[1] See 'Hallucinations of the Self', *British Medical Journal*, 30 July, 1955.

and this Copy, Echo, or living picture' – a subterranean inhabitant wearing human disguise – 'goes att last to his own Herd. It accompanied that Person so long and frequently for Ends best known to it selfe, whether to guard him from the secret Assaults of some of its own folks, or only as ane sportfull Ape to counterfeit all his Actions.'

On the whole, though, the subterranean people show very little concern with the welfare of the human species. Their attitude to mankind is capricious and casual; and, in the imagination of Kirk and contemporary believers, they stand for everything that cannot be predicted or explained by the ordinary processes of human reason. Besides inexplicable disorders of the mind, they cause sicknesses that defy all medical remedy, and even, in the shape of *incubi* and *succubi*, trouble the virtuous sleeper with erotic dreams. They personify every fear that darkens the background of our thoughts, every threatening shape glimpsed out of the corner of the eye. They represent the irrational element in human affairs, the obstinacy and blind spite that we seem sometimes to detect in the behaviour of inanimate objects. They recall, under another aspect, Robert Graves's 'Lollocks' and the malevolent 'Gremlins' dreaded by aviators of the Second World War.

The secret commonwealth surrounds the visible world, underlies it, overlooks it, and, according to the caprice of the subterranean people, perpetually encroaches on it. 'Said to be of a midle Nature betwixt Man and Angel', they have bodies far more aetherial than ours, 'somewhat of the Nature of a condensed Cloud, and best seen in Twilight. These Bodies be so plyable through the Subtilty of the spirits that agitate them, that they can make them appear or disappear att Pleasure. Some have Bodies or Vehicles so spungious, thin, and defecat, that they are fed by only sucking . . . some fine spirituous Liquors'; while 'others feid more gross on the Foyson or Substance of Corns and Liquors, or Corne it selfe that grows on the surface of the Earth, which these Fairies steall away, partly invisible, partly preying on the Grain, as do Crowes and Mice; wherefore in this same Age, they were sometimes heard to bake Bread, strike Hammers, and to do such lyke services within the little Hillocks they most haunt.'

There are still fairies who, 'in some barbarous Places', keep up the customs of the remote past 'before the Gospell dispell'd Paganism', and 'enter Houses after all are rest, and set the Kitchens in order, cleansing all the Vessels'. But the useful domestic goblins, who 'goe under the Name of Brownies', seem to have become comparatively few; and, as a general rule, Kirk's subterraneans lead the easy life of a race of aristocratic parasites; for we, the industrious tillers of the soil, 'do labour for the abstruse People, as weill as for ourselves. Albeit, when severall countreys were uninhabited by us, these had their easy Tillage above Ground, as we now. The Print of those Furrous do yet remaine to be seen on the shoulders of the very high Hills, which was done when the champayn Ground was Wood and Forrest'.

The aristocrats of the underworld are restless, erratic and prone to bouts of melancholy; incapable of remaining long in any one place, 'they remove to other Lodgings at the Beginning of each Quarter of the year, so traversing till Doomsday'. Their chameleon-like bodies then 'swim in the Air near the Earth with Bag and Bagadge; and at such revolution of Time, SEERS, or Men of the SECOND SIGHT ... have very terrifying Encounters with them, even on High Ways; who therefoir uswally shune to travell abroad at these four seasons of the Year ...' Their habitations, built in the crannies and crevices of the earth, are described as large and splendid, 'having fir Lights, continual Lamps, and Fires, often seen without Fuel to sustain them'. Thither they transport mortal women whom they have stolen away to suckle their young, and thither bring the essence of the viands they have purloined from the world above, 'there Food being exactly clean, and served up by pleasant Children, lyke inchanted Puppets.'

Nor are they devoid of literary interests, the libraries they keep underground containing not only numerous volumes of abstruse Hermetic lore, but 'toyish books' intended to amuse, which, however – since they are naturally 'silent and sullen'

68

—merely serve to produce 'some Paroxisms of antic cory-
bantic Jolity, as if ravisht and prompted by a new spirit entering into them at that Instant, lighter and mirrier than their
own.' Knavish and deceitful in their treatment of mankind —
with a morbid habit, if they are sociably disposed, of joining
the guests at a funeral feast — among themselves they are
notably factious and quarrelsome; 'these subterraneans have
Controversies, Doubts, Disputs, Feuds, and Siding of Parties.
... As to Vice and Sin, whatever there own Laws be, sure,
according to ours ... they transgress and commit Acts of
Injustice', such as kidnapping wet nurses, stealing infants
from the nursery and substituting changelings. 'For the In-
convenience of their Succubi, who tryst with Men, it is
abhominable' — Kirk is explicit on the last offence: 'in our
Highlands ... there be many fair Ladies of this aerial Order,
which do often tryst with lascivious young Men, in the
Quality of Succubi, or lightsome Paramours and Strumpets.'
Nevertheless, 'for Swearing and Intemperance, they are not
observed so subject to those Irregularities, as to Envy, Spite,
Hypocrasie, Lieing, and Dissimulation'.

The reader will already have perceived that Kirk's subterraneans have remarkably little in common with the fairy-
land portrayed by Drayton and Shakespeare, at a time when
fairy traditions were still strong among the English peasantry,
or with the delicate Rosicrucian sylphs, more self-consciously
revived by Pope. Their temper is saturnine: their manners
are violent. And we get no indication that they are of less
than human size. 'One of them is stronger than many Men';
and the seer whose vision reflects them is conscious, not of a
company of frolicking and tripping dwarves, but of 'a Multitude of Wights, like furious hardie Men, flocking to him
haistily from all Quarters, as thick as Atoms in the Air ...'
They are believed to procreate, according to the human
fashion, and share many, though not all, of the common
human weaknesses, 'not being drenched into so gross and
dregy Bodies, but yet ... in an imperfect state ... having the
same Measures of Virtue and Vice ... and still expecting

Advancement to a higher and more splendid State of Lyfe'. Even the clothes they wear resemble human modes.

Their Apparell and Speech is like that of the People and Countrey under which they live : so are they seen to wear Plaids and variegated garments in the Highlands of Scotland, and Suanochs therefore in Ireland. They speak but little, and that by way of whistling, clear, not rough ... Ther Women are said to spin very fine, to Dy, to Tossue, to Embroyder : but whither it be as manuall Operation of substantiall refined Stuffs, with apt and sollid Instruments, or only curious Cobwebs, impalpable Rainbows. ... I leave to conjecture as I found it.

So far extends Kirk's survey of the secret commonwealth. His pamphlet runs to twenty-one pages, accompanied by a supplement of fifteen; and, although his manner of exposition is almost as eccentric as his Anglo-Scottish system of spelling, it carries the imprint throughout of a lively and inquisitive mind. If Kirk has a parallel in seventeenth-century literature, probably it is Joseph Glanvill, who was born in 1636 and died in 1680, author of *The Vanity of Dogmatizing* (from which Matthew Arnold took the story of his *Scholar Gipsy*) and *Sadducismus Triumphatus*, an invaluable manual of the seventeenth-century witch cult. Friend of the Cambridge Platonist Henry More, and an early member of the Royal Society, Glanvill combined a scientific interest in physical research with an unshaken belief in witchcraft, magic and supernatural visitations.

Like Glanvill's, Kirk's intelligence was moulded by two different ages. Unlike Glanvill, he was destined himself to become incorporated in the world of legend. He must tell Duchray, Kirk had instructed his relation, that only one chance remained of restoring him to the world of men: 'When the posthumous child, of which my wife had been delivered since my disappearance, shall be brought to baptism, I will appear in the room, when, if Duchray shall throw over my head the knife or dirk which he holds in his hand, I may be restored to society; but if this opportunity is neglected, I am lost for ever.' The christening was cele-

70

brated; and a ghostly image of Robert Kirk appeared. But Grahame of Duchray, 'in his astonishment', failed to perform the ritual gesture – cold iron thrown over the captive's head would have broken the spell and left the captors powerless – and Kirk slipped sadly back into the shadows of the under-world. His cenotaph in the churchyard at Aberfoyle and the unpublished manuscript on his study table were now all that remained of this devoted and unfortunate scholar.

'My Admirable Margaret':
The Marriage of
James Boswell

When it first appeared in the dignified Yale edition, Boswell's *London Journal* enjoyed a resounding popular success that did not entirely depend upon its literary and biographical merits. The less dissolute, more melancholy personage, revealed by *Boswell in Holland* and by his accounts of travel in France and Italy, seems to have made fewer friends; and by unsympathetic readers one even heard it asserted that 'the proud Boswell' was at length becoming a bore. Such petulant criticisms, however, betray a strange insensitiveness. To be bored with Boswell (as Johnson might have said) suggests that one is tired of the spectacle of human life. His gigantic self-portrait is probably the most ambitious, certainly the most richly detailed, work of its kind yet attempted in European literature. It was inspired by a passionate devotion to truth that continued to burn brightly for over three decades. Almost everything we know to Boswell's discredit is derived directly from his own writings.

Like the majority of his fellow human beings, the great self-portraitist was an habitual daydreamer. Boswell was apt to dream *aloud*; and his 'interior monologue' has come down to us unabridged and uncensored. But his self-absorption seldom interfered with his extraordinary gifts of observation;

and among his occasional works are some masterpieces of imaginative reportage – his picture of the moribund David Hume calmly confronting the approach of death; the story of John Reid, an unhappy sheep stealer, whom Boswell attended in his last hours; and the description of the sinister Mrs Rudd, whom he sought out at her London lodgings. 'With how small a speck does a painter give life to an eye!' Boswell had already noted; and in his portraits the essential spark of life usually takes the form of some vivid minor detail – the earthy hue of the dying philosopher's skin; Mrs Rudd's flirtatious badinage; the old cloak, borrowed from the family wardrobe, that the condemned man threw over his shoulders as he stumbled miserably towards the scaffold.

His private problems, nevertheless, were usually Boswell's chief subject. He had the Stendhalian habit of planning his existence as if he had been conducting a military campaign; but, whereas Stendhal, despite his numerous misadventures, frequently reverts to a Napoleonic pose, Boswell is the romantic tryo, surprised and delighted by his moments of triumph and not unduly astonished if he is obliged to admit that he has again failed. A particularly strenuous campaign was set on foot when he decided that the time had come to marry; and the sixth volume of the massive Yale series depicts his hopes and fears and anxieties between 1766 and 1769.

To begin with, he discovers that he is desperately enamoured of the gardener's daughter at his father's country house. He respects the gardener, an able and worthy man: his moral principles forbid him to contemplate the seduction of an honest virgin. 'And therefore, in plain words, I am mad enough to indulge imaginations of marrying her.' It is a dangerously exciting episode; and romantic parallels immediately spring to his mind. The 'enchanting creature' is an Auchinleck housemaid. 'When dusting the rooms with my charmer, am I not like Agamemnon amongst the Thracian girls? All this,' he added prudently, 'may do for a summer. But is it possible that I could imagine the dear delirium would last for life?'

The 'dear delirium' did not last. Indeed, it had ceased to

trouble him within the next few weeks. Boswell left Auchinleck to take the waters at a Scottish spa; and at Moffat he met
the kind of woman who always gave his fancy a 'Sultanic'
turn. Mrs Dodds had three children – but retained a delight-
fully juvenile air – and a Scottish accent; but that was excus-
able, accompanied by so much grace and wit. His friend
Temple, then studying for Holy Orders, yet himself a lover
and a man of the world, received a rapturous bulletin. True,
Mrs Dodds was 'ill-bred, quite a rompish girl', debased his
dignity and lacked refinement: but she was also 'very handsome, very lively, and admirably formed for amorous dalli-
ance. . . . Can I do better than keep a dear infidel for my
hours of Paphian bliss?' But Boswell, just as keenly as Proust,
suffered the pangs of retrospective jealousy. His uncontrollable imagination often represented her former lovers 'in
actual enjoyment of her. My desire fails, I am unfit for love.'
Such fiascos sorely tried his nerves; and he would sometimes denounce her as a cunning jade. Then he would repent
of his severity and fall at his mistress's feet. 'Finer feelings'
were all that she wanted. His 'Circe' was an angel: 'her eyes
looked like precious stones.'

Boswell's liaison with Mrs Dodds, who bore him a little
girl named Sally, his second illegitimate child, continued
intermittently throughout the following year. It had not
been, as he freely confessed, a very creditable affair; but he
allowed the story its proper position in the survey of his
sexual and emotional life. Meanwhile 'Paphian blisses' and
the pangs they provoked were overshadowed by a different
set of feelings. She must remember (he informed his future
wife) 'that a disposition to melancholy and the most violent
passion for the family of Auchinleck make a part of my very
existence.' As the heir to an ancient house, it was, of course,
his duty to contract a suitable marriage. But on whom should
Boswell bestow his hand? The gardener's daughter had long
been forgotten; and his fancy ranged to and fro among a
succession of highly eligible prizes, including 'The Heiress',
Lord Auchinleck's choice since her father held estates near by
– but, strangely enough, she came out with the admission

that she did not really love her suitor; Miss Bosville, who was 'vastly pretty' – her family, incidentally, owned some valuable Yorkshire coalmines; and *la belle Irlandaise*, Miss Mary Ann Boyd, 'a young lady just sixteen, formed like a Grecian nymph ... full of sensibility, accomplished, with a Dublin education. ...'

It was in pursuit of Miss Boyd that Boswell visited Ireland during the early summer of 1769; and he was accompanied thither by his sympathetic cousin, Miss Margaret Montgomerie. Thus we come face to face with the future Mrs Boswell, of whom Johnson was to remark that she had the 'mien and manner of a gentlewoman; and such a person and mind as could not be in any place either admired or condemned.' But Boswell undoubtedly admired her, at least while they were still unwed. He had often been carried away by romantic fancies, he wrote after their return from Ireland, describing his interviews with Mary Ann Boyd; 'but my cousin hung on my *heart*. Her most desirable person, like a heathen goddess painted alfresco on the ceiling of a palace in Rome, was compared with the delicate little Miss. Her admirable sense and vivacity were compared with the reserved quietness of the Heiress.'

Margaret Montgomerie's serious features, with her thick, dark eyebrows, long nose and round, expansive, highly coloured cheeks, as they look out from her portrait, may not tempt the modern reader to liken her to a pagan divinity. But it is clear that she loved Boswell, evidently a man who needed to be loved; and although he could not pretend to be faithful himself, he repaid fidelity with lasting gratitude. His 'admirable Margaret' was always – and would always remain – 'my best friend and comforter', forgiving him when he got outrageously drunk, laughing with him over his matrimonial projects:

Often have I thought of marrying her, and often told her so. But we talked of my wonderful inconstancy, were merry, and perhaps in two days after the most ardent professions to her I came and told her that I was desperately in love with another

76

woman. Then she smiled, was my confidante, and in time I returned to herself. She is with all this, Temple, the most honest, undesigning creature that ever existed.

Boswell and Margaret Montgomerie were married on 25 November 1769; and their marriage contract bore the joint signatures of his two great idols, Samuel Johnson and Pasquale di Paoli.

Now the curtain rises upon a different scene, disclosing Boswell as a married man, established in sober domestic state. Is he happy? Well, happy enough to have resolved that he must refrain from getting drunk and picking up girls. Does he persevere in this salutary resolution? More successfully than most of his readers would expect – even on his 'jaunt to London' in the spring of 1772; though one evening as he walks along the Strand, and passes 'a variety of fine girls, all genteely dressed, all wearing Venus's girdle, all inviting me to amorous intercourse,' he admits that he is 'a good deal uneasy', and finds that his vagrant ideas are apt to 'run into their old channels,' and that he is 'indulging speculations about polygamy and the concubines of the patriarchs and the harmlessness of temporary liking. . . .' He is 'really in a disagreeable state'; and only a delightful interview with his reverend mentor Johnson gives him strength to check his lawless passions. They meet at Johnson's house off Fleet Street· 'The sound of his feet upon the timber steps was weighty . . . he had on an old purple cloth suit and a large whitish wig. He embraced me with a robust sincerity of friendship, saying "I am glad to see thee, I am glad to see thee".'

Between 1772 and the autumn of 1774, Boswell was fully engaged with two important undertakings – his efforts to distinguish himself at the Scottish bar and his plans for becoming a modern biographer. 'I have a constant plan,' he announces as early as March, 1772, 'to write the life of Mr Johnson'; and his hero, though not yet informed of the plan, seems both to suspect its existence and to regard it with a favourable eye. Soon numerous passages, afterwards incorporated in the *Life*, appear among his private jottings. As a general rule, when he transcribed them, they underwent surprisingly little change; but it is instructive to compare his original record with his published version of the same episode, and to note how an extended passage, describing a sharp snub that he had received from Johnson, on 15 April 1772, has been abbreviated and toned down. The person snubbed is no longer Boswell; he is merely referred to as 'a gentleman.'

London, nevertheless, much as he relishes its society, now plays a secondary part in Boswell's existence; and Edinburgh, though he sometimes revolts against its humdrum provincialism, is the main background of his social and professional life. But, on one memorable occasion, during August 1773, the ancient city is enlivened by Samuel Johnson's noble presence. He climbs out of his post-chaise at Boyd's Inn in the Canongate, spends three days under Boswell's roof – where Mrs Boswell finds his slovenly habits extremely annoying and disturbing – and allows himself to be whirled away on an adventurous tour around the Hebrides. It is clear that this Hebridean journey, with all the stresses and strains it provoked, leaves Ursa Major's devoted bear-leader in a somewhat nervous and overwrought condition. Before long, he is to be confronted with an even more exacting test.

John Reid looms on Boswell's horizon – the sheep stealer who had been his first criminal client when he made his debut at the Scottish bar. Though guilty, Reid was then acquitted; now, probably innocent, he is accused of having committed a similar crime; and for the next three months Boswell labours night and day to save the unhappy felon's neck. His account of his struggles does credit not only to his literary gifts but to his love of humanity and to his sense of justice. He fails to secure an acquittal: he also fails to obtain a royal pardon. Meanwhile, the humanitarian and the literary observer emerge simultaneously in his remarkable description of visits to the condemned man's cell. Nothing escapes him; every change of expression is carefully analyzed and put on record; and Boswell winds up with a particularly vivid picture of his wretched client's last days. Reid had elected to be hung in white; and 'all in white, with a high nightcap on ... he appeared much taller, and upon the whole struck me with a kind of tremor. . . . He said calmly, "I think I'll be in eternity in about an hour".'

Later, Reid begins to shiver; and his wife pulls off her old green cloak and throws it compassionately round his white-clad shoulders: 'It was curious to see such care taken to keep from a little cold one who was so soon to be put violently to death.' Later again, Reid meets the executioner who awaits him in the hall on the way to the scaffold: 'When he stepped into the hall, it was quite the appearance of a ghost. The hangman ... then came forth. He took off his hat and made a low bow to the prisoner. John bowed his head towards him. They stood looking at each other with an awkward uneasy attention.' Yet, despite the profound sympathy that he experiences for Reid, Boswell is too instinctively the artist to disregard his own feelings: like the victim's attitude and utterances, they are a source of valuable literary material. There are times, indeed, when he seems slightly callous as he follows Reid on his reluctant progress to the gibbet: 'I had by sympathy sucked the dismal ideas of John Reid's situation, and as spirits or strong substances of any kind ... transferred to another body of a more delicate nature, will have more influence than on the body from which it is transferred, so I suffered much more than John did.'

To some extent, he may have spoken truly; the effect of Reid's trial on Boswell's imagination was certainly pro-longed and grievous. Resolution after good resolution is re-ported to have been broken as the year goes by; and poor Margaret, whom he continues to respect and love, bears the brunt of his drunken ill-temper. At home, he is 'monstrously passionate'. This penitent admission occurs on 8 September. Worse happens on the 17th: 'It gave me much concern to be informed by my dear wife that I had been quite outrageous in my drunkenness the night before; that I had cursed her in a shocking manner and even thrown a candlestick with a lighted candle at her.' It dawns on him that, besides being a brutal husband, he is rapidly becoming a tiresome and unruly guest; for, although now and then he is 'really excellent company' – and notes the fact for future reference – drinking, he acknowledges elsewhere, 'never fails to make me ill-bred'; and he wakes next day with the gloomy conviction that he must have cut a sadly foolish figure. But then, Boswell's virtues and Boswell's vices are almost impossible to disentangle. 'Surely,' writes his American editor, 'there is some connection to be noted between a degree of unhappiness, or at least of restlessness on Boswell's part and his usual habit of self-recording. It is no doubt our good fortune that certain strains of dissonance ... were never entirely suspended and were soon to grow stronger again.' His natural restlessness increased; towards the end of his life, it drove him into chronic alcoholism. Yet his excitability and nervous impressionability were but another aspect of Boswell's astonishing literary talents. Thanks to his peculiar blend of strength and weakness, of introspective and objective gifts. he was able, in the tragic decline of his career, to produce his sane and majestic *Life of Johnson*.

The Brontës

❧

There is an air of stillness, suspense and mystery about many early photographs – for example, a well-known photograph of Haworth Parsonage. Taken during the eighteen-fifties, it looks across a forest of crowded tombs that suggest low granite dinner tables, with the parsonage itself peering at us from bleak windows beyond the churchyard wall. A sexton or labourer in corduroy trousers – perhaps the same old man whom Mrs Gaskell observed 'brooding like a Ghoul over the graves, with a sort of grim hilarity' – sits smoking his clay pipe on a slab that occupies the foreground. A young man in frock coat and light waistcoat stands perched upon another. A litle girl with bare arms and her escort in a top hat remain transfixed upon the churchyard path, his left leg advanced, her fingers tucked beneath his elbow. A distant shape wearing a crinoline gazes away from the camera into the incumbent's narrow garden.

Suppose that the moment thus imprisoned for ever occurred at any time before 30 March 1855, the stone box we are examining, closed by a flattish slate lid, its plain frontage pierced by seven uncompromising casements, must almost certainly have sheltered – since they seldom left home – a blind and aged clergyman, the Reverend Patrick Brontë, and his daughter and housekeeper, Charlotte, widely celebrated throughout England as the authoress of *Jane Eyre*. It may be that, at the moment when the shutter fell, Charlotte was involved in one of those tremendous and heartrending scenes which preceded her marriage to her father's former curate, the Reverend Arthur Bell Nicholls – or merely hard at work around that chilly, well-scrubbed house, baking, polishing and ironing.

The development of the Brontës' tragedy is known, at least in its main outlines, to every English reader: how the three sisters grew up at Haworth; went out into the world for a brief space as governesses and pupil-teachers; returned to Haworth where, in the autumn months of 1845, Charlotte rifled Emily's desk, exposed the manuscript of her poems and, at length, with great difficulty, reconciled her to the suggestion that her verses should be printed. The joint collection of poems by Charlotte, Emily and Anne Brontë, concealed under the androgynous pseudonyms of Currer, Ellis and Acton Bell, met with the failure it certainly deserved, if we except a few memorable fragments in Emily's share of the book. But its appearance kindled the spark of ambition, and the three, almost simultaneously, decided to try their hands as novelists. Emily wrote *Wuthering Heights*; Anne, *Agnes Grey*; while Charlotte composed *The Professor*, the prentice-work from which she eventually quarried some of the materials of *Villette*.

Wuthering Heights and *Agnes Grey*, after numerous disappointments, had been accepted for publication by July 1847. *The Professor* was regularly refused – but refused in such kind and encouraging terms by the last firm of publishers to whom it was submitted that Charlotte was emboldened to send the manuscript of a second book to their offices in Cornhill. *Jane Eyre* was published by Smith, Elder and Company on 16 October 1847. No less immediate than the enthusiasm it aroused in critics as perspicacious as Thackeray and G. H. Lewes was the alarm and indignation it provoked in others. Both reactions are easy to understand. Here, for the first time in the history of the English novel, was the portrait of a passionate woman seen clearly through a woman's eyes. True, the heroine declines to overstep the limits of conventional propriety; but her passion is unashamed and she refuses to deny it:

Do you think I can stay to become nothing to you? (demands Jane of Mr Rochester.) Do you think I am an automaton? – a machine without feelings? and can bear to have my morsel of bread snatched from my lips, and my drop of living water dashed from my cup? Do you think, because I am poor, obscure, plain, and little, I am soulless and heartless? You think wrong! – I have as much soul as you – and full as much heart! And if God had gifted me with some beauty, and much wealth, I should have made it as hard for you to leave me, as it is now for me to leave you.

Such a vehement assertion of a heroine's right to love would have startled and disconcerted during the later eighteenth century, at a time when Mrs Thrale's desperate infatuation for an Italian singer caused her to be ostracized by all the 'Bas Bleu Ladies': it was doubly disconcerting in the mid-nineteenth, when reticence and self-suppression were the badges of feminine virtue. We are scarcely surprised to read the harsh terms in which *Jane Eyre* was stigmatized by one femine reviewer, a Miss Rigby, the future Lady Eastlake, who declared that, if Currer Bell's novel had indeed been written by a woman, it must have been produced by one who, no doubt for some very good reason, had 'long forfeited the society of her sex.'[1] In this connection, it is instructive to remember that, although Harriett Martineau had admired *Jane Eyre*, she frankly disapproved of *Villette*, remarking that she did not 'like the love, either the kind or the degree of it....' Charlotte's triumph – and her main offence – was that she described love of a kind and in a degree that, as felt by a woman, had never been described before.

Hence the continued vitality of her book, notwithstanding all absurdities with which the action is entangled. Those absurdities are manifest and manifold. Charlotte's account, romantic yet acrimonious, of how a fashionable house-party descends on Thornfield Hall, headed by that exquisitely pre-

---

[1] Miss Rigby based her suggestion partly on the authoress's lack of moral reticence, partly on her ignorance of the latest feminine fashions, as revealed by the extraordinary *toilettes* that the beautiful Blanche Ingram wears at Thornfield.

posterous personage, the beautiful Blanche Ingram, combines the sentiments of an envious schoolgirl with the narrative style of a nineteenth-century novelette. We must agree, too, that there is something decidedly 'novelettish' about the character of Mr Rochester. He owes a good deal to Lord Byron, whom the Brontës had worshipped in childhood, and much to the dark heroes of the endless early romances with which Charlotte and her brother Branwell had beguiled their winter evenings. He is any passionate yet inexperienced girl's idea of her perfect predestined lover – not handsome but worse, with his 'falcon eye', his 'broad and jetty eyebrows; his square forehead, made squarer by the horizontal sweep of his black hair,' grim and disillusioned, yet capable of chivalrous tenderness towards the woman he respected.

Edward Rochester is something more. By dint of believing in him, the novelist manages, intermittently at least, to transfer her interest to the reader. But he is never real as Jane Eyre is real. For it was upon her heroine that Charlotte, the most self-centred and, in some respects, one must add, the most limited of artists, bestowed her own power of feeling and strength of imagination. Writing of her three mature novels, one is immediately tempted to apply the words 'sincerity' and 'intensity,' only to be deterred by the subsequent reflection that, although they denote literary qualities, they also cover a multitude of egregious literary vices. Novels composed by young women as passionate, sincere and self-centred as Charlotte Brontë often – in fact, as a general rule – prove remarkably inferior. What, in the first place, saved Charlotte was her grasp of the English language, her firm, almost masculine, appreciation of the beauty and flexibility of English narrative prose. The novelist had received her education from sound eighteenth-century models. *Jane Eyre, Villette, Shirley* are at once uncommonly well-written and (to employ a modern reviewer's cant phrase) extraordinarily 'readable' books. The movement of the narrative is simple, straightforward and commendably expeditious; and, when the novelist wishes to condense her effect, to charge some individual passage with a heightened sense of drama, the

change occurs smoothly and naturally. We have no impression of undue effort or unusual artifice; a deeper note seems
to arise from within, spontaneously evoked by the incidents
she is relating or the situations she is describing. Such passages at their best have a peculiar bell-like gravity – for example, where she tells how Jane Eyre, as a child, escapes from
the brutality of her oppressors into the empty frozen park:

I took a book – some Arabian tales; I sat down and
endeavoured to read. I could make no sense of the subject. . . . I
opened the glass door in the breakfast-room : the shrubbery
was quite still : the black frost reigned, unbroken by sun or
breeze, through the grounds. I covered my head and arms with
the skirt of my frock, and went out to walk in a part of the
plantation that was quite sequestered : but I found no pleasure
in the silent trees, the falling fir cones, the congealed relics of
autumn, russet leaves, swept by past winds in heaps, and now
stiffened together. I leaned against a gate, and looked into an
empty field where no sheep were feeding, where the short grass
was nipped and blanched. It was a very grey day; a most
opaque sky, 'onding on snaw,' canopied all; thence flakes fell
at intervals, which settled on the hard path and on the hoary
lea without melting. I stood, a wretched child enough, whisper-
ing to myself over and over again, 'What shall I do? – what shall
I do?'

Every novelist and every poet has characteristic passages, and shows a predilection for certain images and epi-
thets, in which some aspect of his literary temperament is
concisely summed up. The passages most representative of
the genius of Charlotte Brontë usually reflect the state of
exaltation, half agonized, half ecstatic, that is sometimes
bred of loneliness. Charlotte's pride was fostered on solitude;
but it was accompanied, unlike Emily's, by a considerable
degree of worldly egotism. Never, we are told, could this
small, large-headed, hard-featured woman forget her lack of
beauty. She raged, as did Jane Eyre, at the restrictions her
circumstances imposed upon her feelings. But Jane Eyre, in
the upshot, had conquered Mr Rochester; and the strongest
emotion of Charlotte's life, apart from a wild juvenile cult

for her schoolfriend, Ellen Nussey, had been doomed to failure at its inception and was of a kind impossible for her to divulge to the most sympathetic *confidante*.

During her second visit to Brussels, which lasted from January 1843 to January 1844, we now know that she had fallen desperately in love with the director of her *pensionnat*, the middle-aged and happily married Monsieur Constantin Héger; and the discovery of the letters she wrote him after her return to Haworth – 'desolate and loving letters, in which she pleads for a single word, the merest crumb of comfort, no matter how illusory – shows the extremity of suffering into which her passion plunged her. 'It is humiliating (she wailed) to be the slave of a fixed and dominant idea which lords it over the mind!' The publication of these letters in 1913 – their fragments had been retrieved from her husband's wastepaper basket, reassembled and preserved by the prudent Madame Héger – revealed a Charlotte less immaculate, but also far more interesting, than the young woman who appears in Mrs Gaskell's portrait. For a girl so upright, so proud and conventional, so well aware of her physical shortcomings, yet – in spite of decorum and commonsense – so richly endowed with passionate human desires, it would be difficult to imagine a more appalling *impasse*. She learned to hate Madame Héger, who had at first befriended her: hence the brilliant caricature designed in *Villette*; and the Hégers had a family tradition that her farewell to the mistress of the *pensionnat* contained a threat of retribution. '*Je me vengerai!*' she is said to have exclaimed; and certainly she kept her word.

A discussion of a writer's life in relation to his work involves several obvious dangers. It is clear than an important work of literature is rarely, if ever, a direct transcript of experience. But it is equally clear that an artist's inner creative energies (which have their origins in the hidden recesses of his temperament) find their outlet through some contact with the world of reality around him. No artist, however contemplative, however secretive, can be completely self-sufficient. What he brings to the task from within himself is, no doubt, of far greater value than anything the world can give him. But every work of art must have an objective as well as a subjective basis, and must depend for some of its inspiration on a conflict waged between the self, the individual human spirit, and the alien forces that surround it, by which its integrity is threatened, its identity disputed. The causes of the conflict may be apparently trivial; the experience that fires the brain may be slight and vague and passing. But such an experience there must be, if the materials supplied by the artist's consciousness are to achieve concrete aesthetic form in novel, play or poem.

When we are considering the work of the Brontës in relation to the lives they led, we are at once aware how Anne's relative lack of, or incapacity for, adult emotional experience is reflected by the two novels she composed during her brief, placid, pious, not unhappy lifetime. We also notice how Charlotte's abortive, uncontrollable love for Monsieur Héger, and all that it entailed of misery, humiliation and galling self-reproach, gave her an insight into the workings of passion without which the natural intensity of her temperament might have remained hazy and unfocused. Emily's genius, on the other hand, presents a problem than which there are few more exquisitely perplexing in the entire history of literature. Her nature was as passionate as Charlotte's; *Wuthering Heights*, after a slow and hesitant start, achieves an effect of concentrated violence found elsewhere only among the works of the major Elizabethan dramatists. Yet, although the one or two witnesses who knew her personally hint at the fierce emotional life that she appeared to hide beneath a controlled and taciturn exterior, there is no hint that she ever relaxed her control or, outside the limits of her family, ever came into real contact, either pleasurable or distressful, with any other human being.

Bodily innocence may be of little account. In Emily Brontë the mind was virgin too. She had the 'undaunted courage' that William Blake attributed to the state of spiritual virginity. Her disposition, as we see from her poems, had a strongly devotional bent; and, less orthodox and more adventurous than Anne or Charlotte, she had taken the first steps along the shadowy road that, in its latter stages, is said to lead to mystical illumination:

Burn then, litle lamp, glimmer straight and clear –
Hush! a rustling wing stirs, methinks, the air;
He for whom I wait thus ever comes to me;
Strange power! I trust thy might, trust thou my constancy.

and in another poem:

He comes with western winds, with evening's wandering airs,
With that clear dusk of heaven that brings the thickest stars.
Winds take a pensive tone, and stars a tender fire,
And visions rise and change, that kill me with desire.

Through her verse shines the promise of a modern devotional poet, a Vaughan, Crashaw, Traherne or Herbert of the mid-nineteenth century; and everything we know of her through Mrs Gaskell, all that Charlotte remembered and chose to tell us in her prefaces, confirms the impression of Emily as a remote, silent, almost nun-like creature, who could be harsh (as when with her naked fists she inflicted a savage beating on her disobedient bulldog), obstinately uncommunicative (as when during her last illness she refused either to accept attention or to discuss her symptoms), but who lived in a world of her own, rapturous and self-absorbed, rarely allowing an alien footstep to cross her secret threshold. Presumably she loved her sisters – the link was especially close with gentle pious Anne; but we deduce from Charlotte's letters and memorials that she did not often show it. Perhaps they were sometimes afraid of her; judging by Charlotte's remarks on *Wuthering Heights*, Emily's character frequently puzzled and dismayed them; and, when her novel at last appeared, we may hazard that the perplexity they had always felt increased to stupefaction.

How should Emily, who had been far too shy to hold any sort of converse, when it could possibly be avoided, with the local cottagers and farmers, have conceived this amoral and violent story, interspersed with passages of rough-edged

Yorkshire dialect? What could Emily know of a passion that, although it ascended to a wild unearthly climax, at its source, nevertheless, was as physical as thirst or hunger? By what art did she depict the ravening love-hatred that tortured Heathcliff? Charlotte contented herself, rather weakly, with the sophistical supposition that Emily had, in some manner, represented passions she did not understand, adding a note that she herself doubted whether the representation of such passions were really right and proper. She was appalled by the 'horror of great darkness' that seemed to brood upon the narrative. Heathcliff was an indefensible personage; of Catherine, Charlotte observed that 'she is not destitute of a certain strange beauty in her fierceness, or of honesty in the midst of her perverted passion and passionate perversity.' Had Emily lived (she wished to assure herself), 'her mind would have grown like a strong tree, loftier, straighter, widerspreading, and its matured fruits would have attained a mellower ripeness and sunnier bloom. . . .' As it was, she nursed the conviction that her sister's talent or genius had somehow developed on wrong or misleading lines. During Emily's lifetime, had she not confided to her publisher a belief that 'Ellis will not be seen in his full strength till he is seen as an essayist'?

Today, though we discount Charlotte's criticism, we share in her bewilderment. How did Emily write *Wuthering Heights?* A theory has been put forward – to be received with indignant scorn by most admirers of the Brontës – that Branwell was author or part-author; and some interesting evidence has been produced in support of Branwell's claim. Three witnesses, all associates of Branwell Brontë, and all, so far as can be ascertained, intelligent and trustworthy, asserted either that Branwell had read them fragments of a story which they afterwards recognized incorporated in *Wuthering Heights,* or that they had distinguished in the fabric of the book many of the 'weird fancies of diseased genius' with which he used to entertain them. One added that 'Patrick Brontë declared to me, and what his sister Emily said bore out the assertion, that he wrote a great portion of

Wuthering Heights himself. Indeed it is impossible for me to read that story without meeting with many passages which I feel certain *must* have come from his pen'.[1]

Branwell himself – not, it is true, a clear-headed or well-balanced character – writing to a friend in September 1845, announced that he was busy with the composition of a three-volume novel, of which the first volume had already been completed. It has also been pointed out that certain phrases, used by Branwell in his correspondence, are reproduced by the author of *Wuthering Heights* in narrative or dialogue; and, as a solution of the difficulty, E. F. Benson, in his biography of Charlotte Brontë, has suggested that the earlier and clumsier part of the book may be from the hand of Branwell, but that the more characteristic later passages should be attributed to his sister's visionary genius, which imparted to a coarse and turbulent narrative something of the imaginative ardour we detect among her poems; that Branwell supplied a practical groundwork, his knowledge of men and passions, which Emily then combined in a splendid and lasting structure.

This hypothesis deserves examination. It would be unwise to attach too much importance to the clumsiness of the book's construction or to the inequalities of its prose style. But the Brontës were experienced collaborators; and there is nothing intrinsically improbable in the theory that, just as Charlotte and Branwell during their youth had produced the 'Angrian' chronicles, and Emily and Anne to the close of their lives were occupied with the interminable 'Gondal' histories, Emily and Branwell – after the family scapegrace had finally fallen from the censorious Charlotte's favour – may have collaborated in an adult romance that had for its setting the familiar Yorkshire moors, on which Emily had walked alone, and Branwell had drunk and talked endlessly and brilliantly wherever fortune flung him.

In another respect, they may well have collaborated, Branwell contributing not only ideas and scenes and scraps of local dialogue, but the example of his tragedy. During the

[1]Francis H. Grundy in *Pictures of the Past*.

summer of 1845, on the eve of that period of prodigious literary activity which produced *Wuthering Heights*, besides *Agnes Grey* and *The Professor*, Branwell returned to Haworth, once again in disgrace, having been dismissed from his tutorship in the family of a Mr and Mrs Robinson. He loved Mrs Robinson: he believed that she loved him.[1] 'We have had sad work with Branwell ever since (wrote Charlotte to Emily Nussey). He thought of nothing but stunning or drowning his distress of mind. No one in the house could have rest.' And till his death in September 1848, Branwell's miserable presence continued to haunt the Parsonage, its 'scourge' and its 'drawback', its 'skeleton behind the curtain,' hurrying down to the 'Black Bull' to get drunk on brandy-and-water, stumbling home up the cobbled street to arouse the distracted household with his ravings and his imprecations.

He did not outlive his passion which, assisted by tuberculosis and the supplementary demons of alcohol and laudanum, finally destroyed him. Meanwhile he seized any and every pretext to 'throw all about him into hubbub and confusion,' till Charlotte – doubly unforgiving since she was conscious of the strength of mind with which she herself had faced and surmounted a somewhat similar misfortune – began to loathe and despise her once delightful brother, and Anne, in *The Tenant of Wildfell Hall*, felt obliged to compose a solemn little lecture upon the evils of intemperance. Emily's attitude was less inhuman. She alone would seem to have understood something of the true bitterness of Branwell's tragedy, and to have continued to befriend him in the teeth of Charlotte's hatred. Her affection is expressed in a long obituary poem, evidently intended for Branwell and the last she ever wrote, a lament for spoiled hopes and dissipated powers, for the pilot 'too confiding' in the promise of sea and

[1] Branwell's version of the affair is given in a letter to his friend, F. H. Trundy, whose reminiscences also contain Branwell's assertion that he had written 'a great portion of *Wuthering Heights*.' His affection and admiration for Mrs Robinson, says Branwell, 'led to reciprocations I had little looked for. During nearly three years I had daily "troubled pleasure, soon chastized by fear." '

sky, thrown up at last on a desolate unfriendly shore. Branwell, like Heathcliff, was a victim of hopeless love.

It does not follow that Heathcliff *is* Branwell, or that there was a close resemblance between that rugged, indomitable personage and the nervous, talkative, bespectacled young railway-clerk and tutor, with his ashen face and 'mass of red, unkempt, uncut hair, wildly floating round a great, gaunt forehead,' who passed his happiest days dazzling local topers by the brilliance of his conversation and presiding over the 'Lodge of the Three Graces' in the parlour of the 'Black Bull.' But it is tempting to conclude that a spectacle to Charlotte merely repusive, to Emily was impressive. Branwell's confidences, the sight of his despair, the ravings of misery and remorse that echoed through the Parsonage, may have provided the stimulus Emily's imagination needed – have dropped into the artist's mind a hint that it could work upon, the idea of an irresistible and self-destructive love, a glimpse of Venus attached to her prey with all her teeth and talons.

Otherwise we must accept the enigma; unless new evidence is produced, though we may speculate and suggest, we can never hope to solve it. *Wuthering Heights* was published, together with *Agnes Grey* during December 1847, and was discussed by some reviewers as an immature work by the author of *Jane Eyre*. Meanwhile the disease that undermined the whole family was making rapid progress. Emily, reserved and intractable to the last, succumbed during December 1848, less than three months after Branwell; Anne died on a visit to Scarborough at the close of the following Spring; only Charlotte remained, possessor of a literary reputation that still embarrassed and alarmed her. Anne she had loved and understood. But she was conscious of a deep gulf between herself and Emily, who had stood out always as an exceptional being in the company of her brother and sisters; and, though that dissimilarity must be apparent to the most superficial modern critic, it is not easy to define the difference or to explain how two writers, sprung from the same stock, brought up from childhood in daily association, could have contrived to develop along completely separate courses.

Jane Eyre, is a commonplace book – commonplace, that is to say, in theme and point of view and treatment – carried to success by an extraordinary strength of feeling. About *Wuthering Heights* there is much that is faulty, but little or nothing that is commonplace. The mistakes Emily Brontë made were nearly always technical. She blundered in her method; the most elementary devices are employed to fit story into story; the flow of the first chapters is interrupted by the use of pompous archaistic phrases. But, unlike Charlotte, she rarely erred in the presentation of her subject. The influence of a single personage runs through every chapter. Heathcliff is omnipresent. 'The worst of it is (wrote Charlotte sadly) something of his spirit seems breathed through the whole narrative. . . . It haunts every moor and glen, and beckons in every fir tree of the Heights.' A biographer has suggested that the difference between Emily and Charlotte was, ultimately, the difference between genius and talent. But then, 'talent' and 'genius' are deceptive words, for which no critic has yet supplied a satisfactory definition. The real contrast depends not so much on a difference in artistic ability as on a dissimilarity of aim and of literary point of view.

Emily had the purer, Charlotte the worldlier gift. Charlotte's novels recognize established social values; they are based on minute observation of the people she had known and the places she had visited; they are coloured by her own ambition and pride and amazing moral stubbornness. They belong to a world where money is earned, positions are improved and happy marriages contracted; where obscure merit must fight for a place in the sun, but, after sufferings and vicissitudes, may sometimes hope to climb there. Emily's connection with the world of mundane rewards and conventional retribution is so slight and elusive as to be practically nonexistent. Jane Eyre is a product of the nineteenth century, of its mixture of shrewdness and high-mindedness, its mercantile commonsense and overflowing idealism; Heathcliff (though his death is supposed to occur during the last years of the reign of George III, and he has plainly something in common with the heroes and desperadoes of English romantic verse) exists on a plane fabulous and legendary rather than historical.

To this extent he is a poetic creation; yet the impression he leaves on a reader's mind is never merely abstract. One of the most admirable features of Emily's book is the skill with which she marries the human and the superhuman, and weaves fantastic excesses of feeling into the prosaic familiar pattern of everyday existence. Few novelists would seem to have laboured less over appropriate setting and lighting; yet Wuthering Heights itself – the 'house,' or front room, with its 'vast oak dresser' and 'ranks of immense pewter dishes,' the back kitchen where Hareton skulks and Joseph sermonizes – forms in retrospect an essential part of Catherine's and Heathcliff's story. Then there is the distant brook that murmurs through certain moving passages – 'at Wuthering Heights it always sounded on quiet days following a great thaw or a season of steady rain' – and there is the mysterious cave under Peniston Crag in which Catherine makes believe to Nelly Dean that she sees her gathering elf-bolts. Nowhere is landscape directly described; but its details occur and recur in the characters' dreams and memories.

If Heathcliff is a demon, he is decidedly an earth-bound demon. His creator had a pagan love of the earth; and, although, according to Charlotte, Emily remained all her life a devout and orthodox believer – Branwell, on the other hand, was apparently a sceptic – in *Wuthering Heights* the Christian conception of good and evil is, from the beginning to the end of the story, almost completely disregarded. Heathcliff at the last obtains the only reward that he had ever hoped for. He dies happy, in the embrace of the phantom whose 'little, ice-cold hand' Lockwood at Wuthering Heights hears knocking on the window and grasps in his own when he smashes down the lattice:

His eyes met mine so keen and fierce, I started; and then he seemed to smile. I could not think him dead: but his face and throat were washed with rain; the bedclothes dripped, and he was perfectly still. .... I hasped the window; I combed his black long hair from his forehead; I tried to close his eyes; to extinguish, if possible, that frightful, lifelike gaze of exhultation. ....

Of the novels produced by the Brontës, Anne's *Agnes Grey* and *Tenant of Wildfell Hall* are obviously the least important. Everything that Charlotte wrote has a certain touch of genius, some sonority of expression or depth of imagination; whereas Anne is interesting – primarily, if not exclusively – in relation to her sisters. Her achievement and personality were of the plainest and soberest stuff. She enjoyed writing: she was industrious: she wrote, as one imagines she sewed, methodically and neatly; but her constitution was too well-ordered and far too limited to leave any room for that redeeming unrest from which, given executive power, a work of art is sometimes born. She was the least exciting of the three; yet our comprehension of the family would be incomplete without her. For she represents, so to speak, the raw material of talent, uncomplicated by the additional gifts that tormented Emily and Charlotte; and at her side their achievement seems doubly strange and memorable – strange as that the desperation of Jane Eyre and the agonies of Heathcliff should have been conceived between a graveyard and a cobbled village street, in a cramped sitting-room, behind the blank grey walls of a mid-Victorian parsonage.

Vanity Fair

❦

Next to downright neglect, a so-called 'success and esteem', when everybody praises a book and nobody seems inclined to buy it, is one of the most exasperating experiences that can overtake a hard-worked writer. 'With all its unquestionable success,' complained Thackeray in January 1848, *Vanity Fair* was still not selling, though the first of its yellow-wrappered instalments had appeared just twelve months earlier. Yet, at the same time, it continued to be favourably received. Even the *Edinburgh Review* published an appreciative notice. Mr Thackeray, announced another journal, was 'the Fielding of the nineteenth century'; and Leigh Hunt drew the same comparison; while Jane Carlyle, not the kindliest of women or the least captious member of her literary circle, remarked that, in *Vanity Fair*, Thackeray had beaten Dickens hollow.

Then its fortunes changed; and, before the last instalment had reached the hands of the public – a double number, including chapters sixty-four to sixty-seven, which came out in July 1848 – the despondent novelist felt obliged to admit that he was now 'a sort of great man', and 'all but at the top of the tree', where the author of *Dombey and Son* (serialized between October 1846 and April 1848) was his only genuine rival. At the top he remained so long as he lived; and *Vanity Fair*, he often asserted, was the finest book that he had ever written.

Yet its genesis had been somewhat haphazard. A preliminary draft, entitled *Pen and Pencil Sketches of English Society*, composed early in 1845, was rejected by the publishers; and, though Thackeray had afterwards recast and considerably enlarged his plan, the title he finally chose did not occur to him until the latter months of 1846, when he was staying at Brighton and suddenly leapt from his bed, exclaiming 'Vanity Fair, Vanity Fair, Vanity Fair' while he rushed around his hotel room. Perhaps the title, once he had discovered it, helped to crystallize his scheme of writing. Into the production of *Vanity Fair*, as into the production of almost every masterpiece, there entered an element of happy chance, which combined with the data that the novelist had gathered from life to form a solid literary whole.

In January 1847, Thackeray was a man of thirty-five. He had already suffered much. Some six years earlier, his marriage had collapsed – the wife whom he had loved and done his best to protect had been pronounced a hopeless lunatic; and he was just embarking on his deepest emotional experience, the period of 'longing passion unfulfilled' that was to overcloud his middle age. Yet *Vanity Fair* contains no self-portrait, nor do the incidents of the story bear any close resemblance to the storyteller's own adventures. His book is a synthesis, however, of all his most intense emotions and most strongly held convictions; and it reflects Thackeray, the artist-moralist, from half-a-dozen points of view.

During the Victorian age, it was considered in some quarters not only a socially subversive but a morally disturbing novel. Thackeray's picture of London society, wrote a contemporary *grande dame*, was far 'too accurate to be good for young girls'; and, as late as the beginning of the present century, my mother was forbidden to read it while she lived beneath her father's roof. Once she had left home, she immediately purchased a copy; and this, I suppose, was the small Edwardian volume, with tissue-thin pages and limp green covers, that I read and pondered in my childhood. Since then, I doubt if I have re-opened *Vanity Fair* more than four or five times. Certainly, when I re-read it the other day, I found that I had forgotten almost everything about the tale, except, of course, for its major outlines and a few particularly salient episodes, such as Becky's departure from Chiswick Mall and Rawdon's disastrous discovery of her illicit attachment to the wicked Marquess.

Yet how quickly it regains possession of the mind, and how wide the vistas that it opens! Thackeray was, among much else, a master of the panoramic prospect; and here, from the contrasted fortunes of a group of struggling, aspiring families, he builds up a magnificent panorama of the early-nineteenth-century English life, the life of middle-class 'ready money society' that was beginning to make its appearance towards the close of the Napoleonic Wars. The story opens round about the period of the novelist's birth and infancy, and reaches a climax in 1815, with the Battle of Waterloo, when he himself was not quite four years old. But we are constantly reminded that the society that was then developing would form the basis of mid-Victorian Britain; that little has changed for the descendants of the Sedleys and the Osbornes; and that, when Thackeray writes of Vanity Fair, he is thinking primarily of his own age.

Both as an historian and as a social critic, Thackeray, it must be admitted, had certain obvious limitations. His picture of Regency England, based on his examination of contemporary letters and memoirs, though lively and brilliantly entertaining, is a rather sketchy piece of work; and it is his perfervid interest in the problems of personal life, in the waxings and wanings of love and the rise and decline of friendship, that lends his novel its artistic unity. Not that the novelist sets out to analyse character, or follow the lengthy development of some spiritual or intellectual crisis. Having learned his trade in the school of Fielding and Smollett, he is usually content to fix his personages by the use of bold, dramatic strokes. His subtleties – and he is sometimes surprisingly subtle – arise from his instinctive appreciation of the human mind and heart; from the affection he cherishes for some of his men and women, and the vehement hatred he conceives for others. Few English novelists have ever been less detached; and Thackeray's passionate involvement with his puppets supplies the motive-power that keeps his story flowing.

His attitude towards his feminine personages is a subject that deserves especial notice. Evidently it was by no means straightforward; and the ambivalence of the emotions that he felt for women appears in certain curious turns of phrase. The most disconcerting of these verbal tricks is his obsessive employment of the word 'little', which he attaches, in and out of season, to any woman who awakes his interest, whether it be the half-horrified, half-delighted regard that he feels for Becky Sharp, or the warm, yet slightly disdainful affection aroused by poor Amelia Sedley. A male novelist's view of his own sex may be derived from a number of secondary sources; but, when he is writing of women, he is inclined to depend upon his store of private recollections. In all the women he describes a series of archetypal forms persist – perhaps the masterful mother who dominated his youth, or the elusive unattainable girl who tantalized his early manhood.

Thackeray's wife, we know, was physically a little woman; and her littleness seems to have been a feature that her husband had always found appealing. A pencil-sketch, executed by Thackeray during their early married life, and reproduced by Dr Gordon N. Ray in the first volume of his excellent biography, shows them walking down a London street. William, who was six foot three high and, at least as a middle-aged man, weighed well over two hundred-and-twenty pounds, literally towers above his small companion. His right hand is firmly grasping hers; and, a huge tasselled stick beneath his left elbow, he leads her as he would a child.

It is a charming family portrait, with tragic undertones. Isabella Thackeray, whose nicknames were 'Tobey' and 'Puss', and whom a friend had described before her marriage as 'a nice, simple, girlish girl', was destined to remain a child at heart. Thackeray's affection for his child-wife was always coloured by a shade of patronage, During his courtship, he declared that he had reached a wild 'pitch of sentimentality', which deprived him of sleep and appetite, 'for a plain girl without a penny in the world'; and, once they were married, he still referred to her as 'that diminutive individual' and 'an anxious little soul', perpetually busy and preoccupied and vexed by her domestic duties; though the stews she made tasted of water and onions, and her household accounts, like those of David Copperfield's child-wife, very soon degenerated into hopeless hugger-mugger.

Similarly pathetic was the eventual collapse of her reason. Thackeray had married Isabella Shawe in August 1836; and three daughters had been born to them, one of whom died in infancy. The birth of her last child, Harriet, though her confinement was neither long nor difficult, somehow shattered the young woman's health. She began to experience a vague depression of spirits; and this 'lowness' presently took the form of self-destructive melancholia. In the autumn of 1840, during a voyage to Ireland, the 'poor little woman' actually attempted suicide, and was only saved from drowning by the buoyancy of her mid-Victorian petticoats. 'She was found floating on her back', Thackeray wrote to his mother, 'paddling with her hands, and had never sunk at all. . . .'

He had now to face the fact that the woman he had married was a victim of 'absolute insanity', and that his married life was at an end. Yet he himself was not yet thirty years old, large, robust, athletic, virile, with 'a great fund of animal spirits' constantly bubbling beneath the surface. He enjoyed his bohemian masculine friendships; but he also needed women's company; and in the year 1846 he found that he was growing more and more enamoured of the wife of his old friend, William Brookfield.

By any standard, ancient or modern, the Brookfields were a strange pair, both of them brilliant, both of them ill-balanced, separately attractive yet, as a married couple, mutually competitive, each the centre of a small devoted group over whom they kept a jealous hold. Of William Brookfield, when he was an undergraduate, his acquaintances used to say that he might have been a great actor. His wit is reported to have been 'indescribable'; he was, at the same time, 'a very handsome youth'. He was obliged, nevertheless, to enter the Church, in which, as a modest London curate, he could neither charm nor shine; and even his marriage with a clever and beautiful girl seems to have done nothing to relieve a general sense of disappointment.

As for Jane Brookfield, like so many Victorian women, she had developed a mysterious psychosomatic malady, and retired to a comfortable drawing-room sofa, where she lay, elegant, lovely and languid, and received a few admiring intimates. None of her platonic courtiers was more attentive than Thackeray. 'Mrs Brookfield is my beau-ideal', he informed his mother in 1846. His affection for Jane was a kind of 'spiritual sensuality'; 'her innocence, looks, angelical sweetness and kindness charm and ravish me to the highest degree; and every now and then ... I burst into uncouth raptures', he told her mildly flattered husband.

In the genesis of Thackeray's greatest novel, his unsatisfied passion for Mrs Brookfield obviously played an influential part. While he worked on the text, he admitted that Jane was contributing some details to his portrait of Amelia Sedley; though Amelia is a decidedly foolish woman, and the letters, in which Jane discussed her feelings, her melancholy and the precarious state of her health, reveal a notably keen intelligence. Perhaps it would have been more accurate to say that, although Jane did not resemble Amelia, there were times when Thackeray saw his own predicament – his state of 'longing passion unfulfilled' – in the unhappy plight of Major Dobbin.

Besides the wife whom he had lost, however, and the platonic mistress whom he could not hope to win, a third woman may have had an important effect on his emotional development. Thackeray's father, the prosperous Anglo-Indian, had died when his son was four years old; but his mother, who had married *en deuxième noces* an amiable non-entity named Captain Carmichael-Smyth, continued to take a determined interest in her only child's affairs, watch over his domestic existence and, so far as she could, superintend the whole family. Mrs Carmichael-Smyth is said to have been one of the most beautiful women of her day. She remain puzzling, imperious, romantic. During his boyhood he had worshipped her, wrote Thackeray in later life. Now he saw her through slightly clearer eyes – but 'O so tender so loving so cruel'.

Thus, for the novelist, there were two kinds of women – dominant women, 'women of spirit', like his attractive and possessive mother, and women, like his humble, submissive wife, to whom he often fled for refuge. In *Vanity Fair* he pictures both types – Becky Sharp, eminently the *maîtresse femme*, and her natural victim, poor Amelia – and from their divergent characters and careers produces an absorbing play of contrasts. Thackeray certainly loved Amelia; but he could not help admiring Becky. 'Women of spirit', whatever their moral or immoral qualities, never ceased to fascinate him; and in 1830, on a holiday visit to France, afterwards described in an essay entitled *Shrove Tuesday in Paris*, he had encountered just such a feminine character as excited his imagination and, it may be, stirred his senses.

At a Shrovetide masked ball, a solitary woman, 'about five-and-thirty years of age ... dressed ... in a blouse and a pair of very dirty white trousers', had tapped his shoulder, greeted him by name and asked the shy young man from Cambridge if he did not recognize her. It then turned out that they had already met when she held the position of governess in 'a very sober, worthy' English household; yet 'here she was as mad after the Carnival as the rest, and enjoying herself along with the other mad men and women'. The acquaintance had ripened. Thackeray, for whom she sewed some shirts, often accompanied her to her squalid seventh-floor attic room, where she described her life – and why she had adopted it – 'with the utmost simplicity, and without the slightest appearance of confusion.'

She might well, she said, have decided to stick to her post, enjoyed the advantages of 'a comfortable hot joint every day, with the children, in the nursery, and passed the evening deliciously in the drawing-room, listening to the conversation of the ladies. . . . She might have laid by a competence ... or have seized upon a promise of marriage from young Master Tom, at college. . . . But no. A grisette she was, and a grisette she would be; and left the milords and miladies, and *cette triste ville de Londres* . . . for her old quarters, habits, and companions, and that dear gutter in the rue du Bac. . . .'

This indomitable grisette, Dr Ray suggests, must have lingered in his memory, and may perhaps have been hovering behind him when he created the character of Becky Sharp. Much as he distrusted Becky and everything she symbolized, he could not deny that she had unlimited courage and charm, and a spirit of valiant independence that almost made up for her total lack of virtue. Becky sometimes pretends that, given financial security, she could have been an honest woman:

'It isn't difficult to be a country gentleman's wife', Rebecca thought. 'I think I could be a good woman if I have five thousand a year. I could dawdle about in the nursery, and count the apricots on the wall. . . . I could go to church and keep awake in the family pew; or go to sleep . . . with my veil down. . . . I could pay everybody, if I had but the money.

She was wrong, of course: Becky could never have conformed. Brought up in a hard school, among her drunken father's friends, carry'ng about with her, so long as she lives, 'the dark secrets of those early tainted days', she was cut out to be a life-long rebel. And it is as a born rebel, the type of inveterate recusant, that she weaves her destructive path through the pages of *Vanity Fair*.

In another respect, too, Thackeray's anti-heroine is a solitary, rebellious figure. She refuses to love; possibly she cannot love. Never once does she allow herself to be subdued by an overwhelming human passion. Dobbin loves Amelia; and Amelia loves George. Even Rawdon, the selfish and callous guardsman, falls head over heels in love with Becky; while both Rawdon and Amelia are deeply devoted to their only sons. Becky alone refuses to give an inch; like Shakespeare's Iago or Richard III, she is a resolutely solipsistic character.

Of the various themes that unite in *Vanity Fair*, love is by far the most important. Thackeray pursues it to an extremely cynical conclusion. Love, he decides, is almost always selfish; and here again his personal experience seems to have helped him shape his story. Just as George Osborne callously neglects

Amelia, so Thackeray believed that, during the early days of their marriage, he had himself neglected Isabella; he would often escape from their sadly disorganized household to enjoy an evening of bohemian 'jollifying' or the comforts of his well-appointed club.

In Chapter 29, as he prepares to leave for battle, George gazes down upon his sleeping wife. 'Good God! how pure she was; how gentle, how tender, and how friendless! and he – how selfish, brutal, and black with crime! Heart-stained and shame-stricken, he stood at the bed's foot. . . .' At this moment, Amelia, though 'she wasn't what you call a woman of spirit', appears to be the personification of feminine purity and gentleness. Yet, by Chapter 66, she has been revealed as the virtuous egotist par excellence. She cannot love Dobbin; but she will not let him go: 'He had placed himself at her feet so long that the poor little woman had been accustomed to trample upon him. She didn't wish to marry him, but she wished to keep him. She wished to give him nothing, but that he should give her all. It is a bargain not unfrequently levied in love.' Their union, when Dobbin at length achieves it, fails to bring him lasting happiness.

After love, Thackeray's theme is money, by which nearly every character he introduces is shown as more or less enslaved. For Becky, it is both the basis of social virtue and the master key that will open any door. His riches freeze old Osborne's heart; the loss of the fortune he has earned reduces his rival, Sedley, to a state of drivelling decrepitude. Thackeray's aristocrats cannot despise money – witness his splendid picture of the Bareacres; though, thanks to their hereditary eminence, they can still afford to cut or snub the hopeful parvenus they have encouraged and exploited. During his lifetime, money was gradually breaking down the barriers between the classes. But it had not yet completely done its work; and, when old Miss Crawley's carriage drives northwards to Russell Square from her pleasant house in Park Lane, her coachman and footman feel that they are visiting a foreign country.

As I have suggested elsewhere, Thackeray's vision was intensely personal. His observations are always coloured by passionate sympathy or intense antipathy; and he has the Victorian habit of buttonholing his readers and apostrophizing them in lengthy and eloquent paragraphs. Such was the enthusiasm with which he wrote that he frequently overlooked a faulty sentence; and now and then he makes an odd mistake. There is some confusion about the colour of Becky's hair – was it tawny, 'sandy', red or yellow? – while Miss Crawley's lapdog, elsewhere 'a wheezy Blenheim spaniel', in Chapter 19 temporarily becomes a poodle. His historical details, too, are apt to be incorrect. 'Soda-water was not invented yet,' Thackeray informs us after describing Jos Sedley's drunken jaunt to Vauxhall; though, as his poems and biography demonstrate, Byron consumed it in enormous quantities.

None of these slips seriously impedes his narrative – all his main characters are perfectly consistent beings. Thackeray was both a moralist and a fatalist; he does not pretend that we can ever hope to escape from the limitations of our own inheritance. He was not an orthodox Christian, despite his earnest efforts to preserve 'a beautifully simple faith'. According to his daughter, he regarded the Bible as 'a collection of oriental fables and histories', but said that 'St John was a gentleman', and that he 'liked the Epistle of St James the best', adding 'that it would almost seem as if the . . . stupidity of the disciples had been purposely exaggerated. . . . They were always asking stupid questions.'

Most of the virtues he prized were summed up for Thackeray in the Victorian idea of 'gentlemanliness'; and his views on sexual morality had a social and utilitarian, rather than a Christian origin. Certainly he fretted against the literary restrictions imposed by the current moral and religious code. He regretted that he could not write more freely; since the death of Fielding, he observed, 'no writer of fiction among us has been permitted to depict to his utmost power a MAN'. It was impossible, remarked Walter Bagehot, to read Mr Thackeray's novels 'without feeling that he is perpetually treading as close as he dare to the borderline that separates the world which may be described in books from the world which it is prohibited so to describe'. Thackeray, said Rudyard Kipling later, had the bit of Victorian morality in his mouth, 'and champed on it uneasily'.

Yet, although he may often have suffered a sense of constraint – were he to give a full account, he admits in *Vanity Fair*, of Becky's 'proceedings during the couple of years that followed after the Curzon Street catastrophe, there might be some reason for people to say this book was improper' – it did not prevent him from portraying a thoroughly amoral woman. Becky is portrayed, moreover, with a rare degree of understanding; even she, who has made so many victims, is herself a victim of her circumstances, the product of 'those early tainted days' that had fatally deformed her adult life. Moreover, he manages to convey her charm. Only once does he dwell on her physical attributes – 'green eyes, fair skin, pretty figure, famous frontal development', notes the vulgar Dr Squills. Yet, by describing the extraordinary power she exercises, he is able to bring out all her sexual potency; and here his hints are probably just as effective as the modern novelist's unblushing candour.

How much did we lose through Thackeray's careful reticence? Probably less than a reader at first supposes. True, it would be instructive to learn whether Becky – a suggestion I heard advanced not long ago by a perspicacious female critic – was essentially a frigid woman; and why George Osborne's relationship with Amelia left that lusty young man so bored and restive. But again Thackeray's hints take us a long way. A man of the world who, both before and after his marriage, had lived a cheerfully bohemian life, he knew all that he needed to know of Mrs Crawley and her kind; and, although on some of her 'proceedings' he had decided he must drop the veil, that knowledge is always implicit in his delineation of her moral character.

Dickens' modesty is a great deal more obstructive. With all his literary reservations, Thackeray had never been a false prude; he would not shed tears over the ideal of feminine innocence and simultaneously seduce an Ellen Ternan. The two great writers were natural antagonists; and, although for some years they had presented a semblance of amity, in 1858, when Dickens deserted his wife, a cantankerous journalist, named Edmund Yates, involved them in a bitter public quarrel from which their understanding never quite recovered. It was Thackeray's notion of what constituted gentlemanly behaviour that had originally provoked the clash. Unlike Thackeray, Dickens was not a 'gentleman' – he was far too showy, exuberant, effusive; while Thackeray retained many of the prejudices and prepossessions of the English upper-middle class.

Their differences extended to the use of language. Whereas Dickens' genius had a decidedly baroque turn, Thackeray was a comparatively sober stylist. Dickens enriches his narrative with long fantastic set-pieces – the wonderful description of a London fog in *Bleak House*, or of the Veneerings' dinner-party in *Our Mutual Friend*. But this kind of unbridled virtuosity was entirely alien to his rival's nature. Thackeray's highest descriptive flights – the pictures of the meet at Queen's Crawley and Miss Osborne's drawing-room in Russell Square – rise gradually from the surrounding text and as quietly sink back again. They show none of Dickens' dark fantasy or his uncontrollable poetic brio.

Yet each had a troubled spirit; and, during middle life, each was distracted by a violent secret passion. Ellen Ternan is said never to have returned the desperate love that she inspired in Dickens – hence the novelist's creation of a series of heartless heroines who bear some variant of her name; and Jane Brookfield, at her husband's demand, finally consented to sever her relations with Thackeray. Her unhappy adorer then discovered that he had lost 'the one good thing' in his existence. He wished that he had never loved her, he cried: 'I have been played with by a woman, and flung over at a beck from the lord and master – that's what I feel. I greet her tenderly and like a gentleman: I will fetch, carry, write, stop – but I leave her.... It's death I tell you between us.' He burned all the tokens she had given him; yet for some days after their separation, still hoping that he might catch a glimpse of Jane, he hung miserable around her London house.

Of Thackeray in later life we have many entertaining sketches; and only Thomas Carlyle produced a definitely unfavourable judgement. 'There is a great deal of talent in him,' he pronounced in 1852, 'a great deal of sensibility – irritability, sensuality, vanity without limit – and nothing, or little, but sentimentality and play-actorism to guide it all with. . . .' Here the self-appointed censor of his age is attacking the chameleon artist. Despite his habit of striking moral attitudes, Thackeray was an imaginative artist first and foremost. He had subtitled *Vanity Fair* 'A Novel Without a Hero'. During its composition, he declared at the time, his chief object had been 'to indicate, in cheerful terms, that we are for the most part an abominably foolish and selfish people . . . all eager after vanities . . . If I had made Amelia a higher sort of woman there would have been no vanity in Dobbin's falling in love with her . . . I want to leave everybody dissatisfied and unhappy at the end of the story. . . .'

We *ought* to be dissatisfied, he adds: our own stories seldom turn out well. Otherwise, though he often scolds and preaches, he refuses to deliver any general message. What really interests him is 'to convey as strongly as possible the sentiment of reality'; and this he does by cutting deep into the complex strata of the nineteenth-century English world, and presenting us with a multitude of different personages, each of whom incorporates a vivid spark of individual life. *Vanity Fair* is an extraordinarily living book. 'The sentiment of reality' persists throughout. It is from Thackeray's response to reality, rather than from his criticism of mankind, that his tale derives its epic character.

Sir John Soane
and His Museum

❦

In my childhood, I possessed a private 'museum' – the name I gave to a small brightly painted wooden box, which contained a flint from an eighteenth-century flintlock gun, a number of old coins, a South American nut, a gold-and-green exotic beetle, odds and ends of Roman British pottery and some ancient clay tobacco-pipes. Though at the time I did not suspect it, my collection had a long and distinguished ancestry, and was formed on much the same principles as many famous collections of the past. Until a comparatively recent period, few museum curators attempted to arrange their exhibits according to a strictly scientific method.

Both Oxford's original Ashmolean, founded with the help of the celebrated antiquary Elias Ashmole in the year 1683, and the earlier Museum Tradescantium, popularly called 'Tradescant's Ark', were designed as, above all else, 'Cabinets of Curiosities'. John Tradescant, for example, was a naturalist and royal gardener, who, having examined the flora and fauna of Europe from Russia to the Balearic Islands, in 1637 visited the American Colonies, gathering wherever he went the precious botanical specimens with which he stocked his garden and his London house. Among the trees and shrubs he introduced to England were the lilac, the acacia and the occidental plane. The descriptive catalogue he presently published shows the diversity of Tradescant's interests. Besides the herbs he grew in his 'physic garden', it lists birds, quadrupeds, fish, shells, insects, mineral specimens, fruits, instruments of war, medals and outlandish costumes.

Such were the curiosities that travellers flocked to see: unfamiliar and beautiful plants: the stuffed carcasses of strange beasts: gaudy shells arranged in pleasing patterns: fragments of metal and stone that recalled the genius of former ages: weapons that illustrated the manners and customs of remote, barbaric peoples – anything, in fact, that stirred the imagination and aroused a sense of awe and wonder. Compared with these early collections, the museum, as it developed during the second half of the nineteenth century, became a kind of scientific warehouse. True, modern curators, their eye on the general public, nowadays often adopt a more attractive mode of presentation. But there are still many scholars who feel that the museums over which they preside should be reserved, so far as possible, for the use of the learned specialist, and that the ordinary visitor is a tiresome intruder, to be tolerated but not unnecessarily encouraged.

Meanwhile, the old 'Cabinets of Curiosities' had been closed and broken up. All except one. In 1813, the renowned architect, Sir John Soane, moved into the house he had built for himself overlooking a pleasant London square, and installed the heterogeneous collection he had gradually been assembling. At No 13 Lincoln's Inn Fields, he established the Museum that was to be his private monument. But, before we consider the monument, we must turn our attention to the man. Sir John Soane's Museum is a remarkable edifice, and bears the imprint of a remarkable personality.

Its founder was born in September 1753, the son of a modest country builder, and at the age of fifteen entered the office of George Dance, whose grim masterpiece was Newgate Prison, where, above the windows, garlands of fetters took the place of the customary classical decorative wreaths. After two years, however, he joined Henry Holland, partner of 'Capability' Brown, the well-known reformer of the English landscape, who owed his nickname to his habit of assuring his employers that their ancestral pleasure-grounds, he felt sure, were 'capable of great improvement'. Next, Soane obtained a scholarship – 'the most fortunate event in my life' – which made it possible to visit Italy; and there he secured a rich and highly eccentric patron, Frederick Augustus Hervey, Bishop of Derry, who soon afterwards added a coronet to his mitre and entered the House of Lords as the 4th Earl of Bristol. 'The Building Bishop' was devoted to architecture; and, under his wing, Soane studied the antiquities of Naples and the temples of Paestum, which left a deep impression on the young man's mind.

Having returned to England, he soon contracted a sensible and happy marriage. Eliza Smith, the niece of a prosperous builder, became his wife in 1784, and bore him two sons, John and George, neither of whom was destined to turn out well. By the middle of the decade, Soane had already begun to make his way; and, in 1788, he was appointed architect and surveyor to the Bank of England, a post he held for forty-five years. Then, in 1790, his wife's uncle died, bequeathing Soane a comfortable fortune. He was now free of economic anxieties and could settle down to develop his own style, which until his death he continued to impose upon a lengthy series of private and official buildings.

Soane's style has been described as 'Romantic-Classicism'; and, although some English writers are inclined to regard his work as merely 'a quaint cul-de-sac ... off the main line of English architectural development', foreign critics, we are told, recognize him as 'one of the greatest English figures in the general late-eighteenth- and early-nineteenth-century artistic movement[1]....' His predecessors had been predominantly English; Soane learned much from Continental theorists – for instance, from the Abbé Pierre Laugier, of whose revolutionary treatise, *Essai sur l'Architecture*, he acquired as many as ten copies. But his method was eclectic; and Gothic and Renaissance motifs were often woven into a classical design. Since his childhood, he wrote, he had been in love with architecture; and, throughout his whole life, he 'pursued

[1]Dorothy Stroud, *The Architecture of Sir John Soane*, 1961; from the Introduction by Professor Henry-Russell Hitchcock.

it with the intensity of a passion'. What he sought was 'the poetry of architecture'; and he attempted to achieve it, not only through the proportions and details of an edifice, but through ingenious effects of lighting. A beautiful structure was to be the realization of a dream, stately and dignified but also somehow strange; and, when his friend F. M. Gandy produced a panoramic drawing of Soane's assembled church designs, he littered the foreground with fragments of antique temples that would have appealed to Poussin or Claude Lorrain, and gave it a background of wild and bosky hills.

Despite his prosperity, Soane was an indefatigable worker, perpetually travelling, sometimes in his carriage, sometimes on foot, and spending seven or eight hours at his drawing-board every day of the week except the Sabbath. His sons, John and George, had disappointed him; and George is said to have broken his mother's heart by publishing an unfavourable reference to his father's talents. During Soane's last period of creative activity, from 1820 to his death in 1837, the 'dear old tyrant' – his enthusiasm wore out the youths he employed – became increasingly remote and odd. Very tall and thin, he was dressed, wrote one of these assistants, 'entirely in black; his waistcoat being of velvet, and he wore knee-breeches with silk stockings. ... It can be scarcely said that he had any front face. In profile his countenance was extensive: but looking at it "edgeways" it would have been "to any thick sight" something of the invisible. A brown wig carried the elevation of his head to the almost unattainable height; so that, altogether, his physiognomy was suggestive of the picture which is presented on the back of a spoon held vertically'.

Thus he appears in Lawrence's portrait; and thus we imagine him, seated at his fireside, shielding his red-rimmed eyes against the blaze, while the same assistant, George Wightwick, read aloud from *Gil Blas*. 'P-o-o-r Gil! p-o-o-r Gil!' Soane would murmur reflectively. Bereaved of his wife, who had died in 1815, saddened by the behaviour of his sons, both of whom made unfortunate marriages, troubled with turbulent romantic visions he could never quite translate into stone and brick, he himself was not a happy man. Yet he had consolations – none more soothing perhaps than the Museum he had built up, which, after his death, through a special Act of Parliament, he bequeathed to his countrymen 'for the benefit of the public'. He was eighty-four when he died, leaving behind a meticulous *Description* of the house in which he had spent nearly a quarter of a century.

Primarily, it is a monument to the owner's taste. Soane had built the house; and he also furnished it, down to such minor domestic features as the grates and fire-irons; while the collection it encloses was carefully arranged to reflect his general frame of mind. At first sight, it is a gigantic magpie's-nest. But, as Professor Hitchcock remarks, there is something 'almost Surrealist' about 'the organized clutter of disparate objects' gathered together in the domed Crypt. J. M. Gandy's rather fanciful water-colour, even more vividly than the existing arrangement, suggests the effect that he intended to achieve. Ledge after ledge lines the walls of a narrow, lofty, shaft-like chamber, running up through the house from the basement to the topmost floor; and walls and ledges and innumerable brackets are laden with broken masses of antique sculpture, bits of capital and frieze and plinth, Roman statuettes and portrait-heads, lion-masks and occasional tombs and vases, all bathed in a dim mysterious glow.

This atmosphere of mystery the architect did his best to evoke even in more modern rooms. He liked to produce an effect of depth, and, whenever he could, contrived a vista; so that, although No 13 Lincoln's Inn Fields is not a very large house, it resembles a romantic labyrinth, offering endless surprises and strange discoveries as the visitor slowly threads its maze. Here is a Gothic fantasy, named 'The Monk's Parlour'; and through its window we glimpse the mediaeval cloister that Soane constructed from the scraps of fifteenth-century stonework he had appropriated while he was restoring the old Palace of Westminister. The 'Catacombs' are full of funerary urns: 'The Sepulchral Chamber' enshrines the sarcophagus of Seti I, removed from the Valley of the Kings in 1817.

There are a 'Flaxman Recess' and a 'Shakespeare Niche'.

'The Picture Room', added in 1824, contains two of Hogarth's finest pictorial series, *The Election*, which is among his noblest achievements, and his earlier representations of the Rake's tragedy. Hogarth and Watteau rub shoulders with Reynolds and Turner, Graeco-Roman marbles with contemporary plaster-casts; places are found for illuminated manuscripts, for a silver watch reputed to have belonged to Sir Christopher Wren, and a jewel said to have been discovered in Charles I's baggage after the Battle of Naseby.

Few men have compressed so much of themselves into so limited a private setting. Monuments are defaced: houses are pulled down. Every year twentieth-century London discards something of its individual quality, as impersonal cosmopolitan buildings break the outlines of old-fashioned streets and squares. But, if Sir John Soane were suddenly to re-emerge beneath the plane-trees of Lincoln's Inn Fields and cross the threshhold of his old house, he would notice very little change. Seti's sarcophagus has lost its blue lining, and its alabaster is now somewhat darkened; the plaster casts are a trifle yellower; the mirrors, so cleverly installed to add a new perspective to the breakfast-room, are growing silvery and dim with age. Otherwise his monument is unspoiled, and likely to remain unspoiled while Acts of Parliament are still honoured. The average museum pays its tribute to the genius of humanity at large. The value of Sir John Soane's Museum does not depend either on the breadth of its scope or on the value of its contents. It is a record of the lifelong adventures of a single adventurer's imagination.

'L'Art Sans Poitrine'

❦

On the last day of December 1886, at the Church of St Barnabas, Addison Road, London, Jules Laforgue, the rising young Symbolist poet, then in his twenty-seventh year, was married to a Miss Leah Lee, a youthful teacher of English whom he had met abroad – 'very thin (he wrote to his sister before the marriage), very, very English, with chestnut hair . . . a childish face, a mischievous smile and great tar-coloured, forever astonished eyes. . . .' Six decades later, the author of *Four Quartets* chose to be married in the same building.

A strange coincidence – and that it was no more than a coincidence I have been assured by T. S. Eliot himself. For Laforgue was one of the literary ancestors who dominated his early poetic life; and, although he was beginning to outgrow Laforgue's influence at the time when he wrote *The Waste Land*, their relationship, while he was still producing such poems as *Prufrock*, *Portrait of a Lady*, *Conversation Galante* and *La Figlia che Piange*, was evidently very close indeed. Here it is worth noticing that Eliot learned French, soon after he left Harvard, from the exquisite novelist Alain-Fournier, and that Alain-Fournier belonged to the select band of those who cherished Jules Laforgue's memory. By comparison (he told Jacques Rivière) he regarded Rimbaud as an 'incomplete genius'. On almost every page of Laforgue's poems he found phrases that perfectly evoked a 'vision' – a vision that exceeded and transcended the actual words the visionary poet had employed.

Considering the influence he exerted in later years, Laforgue's life-span was pathetically brief. His parents were Bretons. Born in 1860 at Montevideo, he returned to France in 1866 and was educated first of all at Tarbes, afterwards at a famous Parisian school. As a youth, he attracted the attention of the well-known art-collector Charles Ephrussi (of whom Proust appears to have made some use while he was elaborating his memorable portrait of Charles Swann); and Ephrussi, besides employing him as his secretary and research assistant, introduced him to the new Impressionist painters and, later, with the help of the fashionable storyteller, Paul Bourget, recommended him for a more remunerative post.

Towards the end of 1881, Laforgue became French reader to the Empress Augusta of Germany, a somewhat fantastic and capricious personage, whom he continued to serve until 1886. But during that year he met Leah Lee, and decided to abandon his appointment and settle down again in Paris – marriage, he thought, would 'prevent waste of time, vague restless moods and create a citadel about the writer'. The following August, alas, he died in his sleep, carried off by an 'obstinate cold' – caught, he believed, as he travelled home across the English Channel – which afterwards proved to be advanced tuberculosis. Latterly, he had been poor and harassed by debt. Leah Laforgue, who had also contracted the disease, died at Menton in 1888.

Such is the simple outline of an extraordinarily active and disinterested career. Unlike his fellow Symbolist, Tristan Corbière, Laforgue never composed his own epitaph. Yet nearly everything he wrote was related to his immediate experience of his life, and many of his finest poems and tales have a vivid autobiographical colouring. Particularly characteristic is the mocking *Avertissement* with which he prefaced *Les Fleurs de Bonne Volonté*:

> *Mon père (un dur par timidité)*
> *Est mort avec un profil sévère;*
> *J'avais presque pas connu ma mère,*
> *Et donc vers vingt ans je suis resté.*

'L'Art Sans Poitrine'

Alors, j'ai fait d'la littérature,
Mais le Démon de la Vérité
Sifflotait tout l'temps à mes côtés:
'Pauvre! as-tu fini tes écritures. . . .'

A romantic *malgré lui* and yet an intellectual cynic, a sensuous lover of life and yet a puritanical idealist, Laforgue did not profess to command an extensive range of literary themes. But those few themes he explores and re-explores with admirable subtlety and pertinacity. He reverances literature, but cannot lose sight of its inherent limitations – he does not imagine, as Rimbaud imagined, that the power of words was capable of transfiguring the earth. He is deeply in love with the idea of love, but is conscious that the idea he cherishes has little reference to the naked physical fact.

In his collection of tales, *Moralités Légendaires*, frustrated idealism is his favourite subject; and the best of these stories, *Lohengrin, fils de Parsifal*, gives the familiar legend an ingeniously sardonic twist; for the Swan Knight, once he has rescued Elsa – a delicious young person, *'nubile à croquer'* – finds that he is expected to marry his beloved; and their honeymoon proves to be an anti-climax that involves the spoliation of all his hopes and dreams. At length the devoted swan answers his desperate appeal, and Lohengrin rides through the window into the freedom of the sky, 'towards the Heights of Metaphysical Love, towards those glacier-mirrors that never a young girl can breathe upon and cloud, tracing with a finger in the steam her name and the date'.

Laforgue's prose is difficult to translate; his verse, in which he achieved his effects, as he mastered the technique of *vers libre*, by using the idiom of common speech and adapting and parodying the refrains of popular songs, sets even the most sensitive translator a practically insoluble problem. So much depends on the peculiar rhythm of his poems, with their melancholy individual music: on the mixture of tenderness and irony that characterizes his view of the humdrum everyday world: lastly, on the poet's choice of subjects, from which he has banished nearly every theme dear to his Romantic predecessors, writing not of mountains and torrents, God, immortality and the fate of Man, but of the thousand-and-one petty joys and sorrows that make up the sum of ordinary human experience. Most poets inhabit a solitude. Laforgue is doubly alone amid familiar sounds and sights – in a hotel room, listening to a distant piano; travelling along a deserted highroad where the telegraph-wires sigh and whistle; in a provincial street when dusk has begun to fall; in a railway station, or beside a quay, from which train or lake-steamer has just departed. For it is in those surroundings that the modern Hamlet comes face to face with his own solitary image, and catches a glimpse of himself as he aspires to be, against the subfusc background of contemporary life as it is:

> *J'aurai passé ma vie le long des quais*
> *A faillir m'embarquer*
> *Dans de bien funestes histoires*
> *Tout cela pour l'amour*
> *De mon coeur fou de la gloire d'amour*
> *O! qu'ils sont pittoresques les trains manqués!* ...

Certainly Laforgue had an exquisite gift, though he worked within rather narrow limits. But then, the limitation of his talents were very often self-ordained. His literary ideal, he said, was '*l'art sans poitrine*' – slender, bosomless art, without rhetorical flourishes or superfluous curves; his muse was to be a nymph, not an exuberant Wagnerian goddess. And it is by the standards he so carefully drew up for himself that we should judge the verse and prose he bequeathed to posterity.

'My Heart Laid Bare'

❦

In her charming and far too little known autobiography, *Le Collier des Jours*, Judith Gautier describes how one day, as a young girl, she looked out of the window of her father's suburban house – it was a gloomy sunless afternoon during the late autumn or the early winter – and saw approaching along the road (which, incidentally, bordered the grounds of a celebrated asylum where many distinguished lunatics had come to spend their last months) a singular procession consisting of a man and a dog. The dog was a large, dejected mongrel, with a tail that dragged behind it. The man, a spare, dandified figure, in a tubular frock coat of tightly fitting black, was following the dog on tiptoe, apparently determined to tread on the end of its tail. Suddenly he succeeded. The dog turned on its pursuer with a yelp of rage or pain; and the man, losing his balance, toppled and fell backwards into a wayside ditch which brimmed with yellow muddy water. Charles Baudelaire was visiting his 'master and friend', the 'perfect magician', Théophile.

It must have been about this period that Baudelaire was introduced to the brothers Goncourt; and admirers of their *Journal* will recollect that, although they have little to say about his work or conversation, they were unfavourably impressed by his personal appearance and by what they hit off in their smart, effective style as his *'toilette de guillotiné'*. Baudelaire was still best known as a satanic *poseur*; and many decades were to elapse before this self-made legend ceased to obscure the irradiation of his true poetic genius.

Only during the present century, now that the influence of

the critics of the 1890s has gradually died away, has it become possible to see Baudelaire in his correct perspective. The element of self-parody and the streak of sensationalism (dubbed by a modern French critic his *'satanisme à bon marché'*) appear less and less important; and we have learned to discount those occasional vulgarities of expression – for example, the *'divans profonds comme des tombeaux'* over which the late George Moore used to hold up pale, plump hands in fastidious disapproval.

There is probably no single collection of verse, published during the nineteenth century, that has stood the test of time better than *Les Fleurs du Mal*. There is none to which we return more often, that preserves a greater air of freshness, and offers more surprises at each successive exploration. Baudelaire's verse, at its finest, combines the delicacy and suppleness of French with something of the brazen sonority of the greatest Latin poets. As Jules Laforgue pointed out in his admirable notes on Baudelaire, printed among the *Mélanges Posthumes*, he added a new and poignant tone to the orchestra of modern poetry: *'Il a trouvé le miaulement, le miaulement nocturne, singulier, langoureux, désespéré, exaspéré, infiniment solitaire. . . .'* Yet how courageously he confronted some majestic commonplace; how boldly he would employ some apparently humdrum phrase!

Il a le premier trouvé (wrote Laforgue) *après toutes les hardiesses de romantisme ces comparaisons crues, qui soudain dans l'harmonie d'une période mettent en passant le pied dans le plat. . . .*

And elsewhere Laforgue comments on:

Cette noblesse immuable qui annoblit les vulgarités intéressantes, captivantes; cette façon de dire – et cela sans périphrase prude, poncive – cette familiarité de martyr entre les plus grands qui peut lui faire dire:
'Les persiennes abris des secrètes luxures' et une page plus loin:
'Andromaque, je pense à vous!'

Baudelaire, however, was not merely one of the most original, eloquent and expressive of nineteenth-century poets: he is also in the front rank of modern prose writers. He believed that a true poet must necessarily be a critic: '... *tous les grands poètes deviennent naturellement, fatalement, critiques. Je plains les poètes que guide le seul instinct; je les crois incomplets.*' A poet must discover the laws that govern his own activities, and must attempt to systematize the enjoyment that he derives from the work of others. '*Je résolus*' he explained at the beginning of his essay on Wagner, '*de m'informer du pourquoi, et de transformer ma volupté en connaissance.*'

Thus it came about that he left behind him, in addition to *Les Fleurs du Mal*, an assemblage of critical essays, unusually solid and well-argued, yet lit up by constant flashes of imaginative insight. That he was sometimes misguided goes without saying. Obviously his cult of Poe was exaggerated, his championship of Wagner partisan. Not all the painters he admired have kept their interest. We prefer today to remember Fromentin as a novelist and author of splendid travel books; Baudelaire's description of a Boudin sunset has more literary charm than the original canvas, one suspects, possessed aesthetic value. He had a good word for Meissonier, and was occasionally indulgent towards Ary Scheffer. Yet, when the reckoning is finally calculated, he emerges with a formidable credit-balance of brilliant observations. His study of Constantin Guys, *Un Peintre de la Vie Moderne*, is surely one of the most astonishing feats of constructive criticism and imaginative interpretation that have ever been accomplished.

But then, the essays were not all. Besides his critical prose, he left to the world the papers that have since been published under the general title of *Journaux Intimes*, and are subdivided into *Fusées, Mon Coeur Mis à Nu* and *Choix de Maximes Consolantes sur l'Armour*. The second, at least, is a sketch for a full-length volume. '*Ah, si jamais*' he declared, '*ce livre ... voit le jour*, Les Confessions, *de J.-J. Rousseau, paraîtront pâles.*' The sketch was never worked up, the outlines never filled in. Yet, even in their fragmentary state, the

Journaux Intimes, particularly *Mon Coeur Mis à Nu*, rank high among modern attempts at critical self-dissection. They are a clue to the development of Baudelaire's mind – there can, of course, be no single clue to the evolution of his genius. At the same time they provide hints of immense importance to our understanding of his period, of the processes of decay and rebirth, the phases of hope and hopeless disillusionment, from which sprang the bewildering fertility of nineteenth-century art and literature.

They reveal a man who hates and fears life, and who hates and despises the conditions of modern society (who is oppressed by an *'immense nausée d'affiches'* and who wonders that an honest man can touch a newspaper without an instinctive movement of repulsion), yet is fascinated by the beauty that lies in squalor, the energy that he seems to distinguish flowering in evil; whose attitude towards the world and his fellow human beings is swayed by alternate impulses of rejection and acceptance. He has an invincible yearning for the life of the spirit, and opens *Fusées* with the affirmation: *'Quand même Dieu n'existerait pas, la religion serait encore sainte et divine.'* But had Baudelaire been born the ascetic he often longed to be, had he never penetrated those labyrinths of sensual experience where he lost health and happiness and ordinary peace of mind, what his character gained in dignity his imagination would have forfeited in richness and variety.

On the one hand, he is an impassioned puritan, with a puritan's distaste for Woman, whom he regards as the natural enemy of the saint or artist; on the other, he is a passionate observer of the contemporary social scene, enamoured of the *'beauté de circonstance'*, *'le beau multiforme et versicolore, qui se meut dans les spirales infinies de la vie,'* a beauty he finds in clothes and equipages; in *'quelque chose d'ardent et de triste'* he glimpses in the face of an unknown passer-by; in the tide of urban prostitution which, as dusk falls and the gas-jets flutter and rustle under the wind, begins to creep like an invading army along the crowded greasy pavements.

To gather and convey these impressions, and maintain all the while a delicate equipoise between equally violent impulses of love and hatred, demands of the poet-critic a very special training. The laborious and painful self-education that Baudelaire underwent is closely connected with his theory of the Dandy. In Baudelaire's scheme of things, the Dandy is no Brummell; for Brummell had his epicene side, and Baudelaire's Dandy is everything that Woman is not and, in his view, owing to her peculiar constitution, everything that she never can be:

> *La femme* (he enunciated in *Mon Coer Mis à Nu*) *est le contraire du Dandy. Donc elle doit faire horreur. . . . La femme est naturelle, c'est-à-dire abominable.*

Here it may be as well to remind his feminist readers that Baudelaire's anti-feminism had, in the last resort, a strongly personal basis. He could not forget or forgive the wound inflicted on his youthful sensibility by his adored mother's remarriage to the dashing General Aupick. Henceforward there existed in his mind an almost unbridgeable gulf between sensual and spiritual love; the women he loved spiritually (as he loved the mysterious 'Marie' and that jovial and commonplace personage, Madame Sabatier) he found it difficult or impossible to approach physically: the earthly Venus was seductive but necessarily abject.

The passage quoted, nevertheless, has also deeper references. Baudelaire's work, both as a poet and as a critic, is a continued protest against *Nature*. In his mythology, as in that of William Blake (whose *Marriage of Heaven and Hell* would certainly have interested him), Nature is the villain. Virtue and beauty are the products of artifice: '*Le mal se fait sans effort, naturellement, par fatalité; le bien est toujours le produit d'un art*'; and, in one of his critical essays, '*C'est bête comme la nature,*' he remarks of a statue by David. True, he was frequently inconsistent. We recall the famous and exquisite sonnet in which he speaks of Nature as a temple up-borne on living pillars, as a 'forest of symbols', full of strange meaning to the man who wanders through its avenues. But poets differ from philosophers inasmuch as they recognize that a conflict, even a confusion, of ideas, if accurately reflected and honestly reproduced, may be as revealing as a hard-and-fast system achieved by ruthless intellectual pruning.

Thus Baudelaire abominates Woman, yet drifts into profound reveries suggested by his mistress's beauty, in one aspect spiritual, in another sensual and ephemeral; he reconciles (or, rather, does not attempt to reconcile) his detestation of Nature, and his avowed preference for landscapes where man predominates, with his devotion to the sea – *'spectacle ... infiniment et ... éternellement agréable.'* Yes, he is inconsistent, variable, capricious. But the object of his notebook-jottings was to lay his heart bare, to chart its troubled and changing responses to the universe around him. Few writers have done so more thoroughly. We cannot pretend that Rousseau's *Confessions*, compared with *Mon Coeur Mis à Nu*, seem pallid and uninteresting. But we feel that they belong to a different world – to a world that came to an end with the Romantic movement. Where Romanticism ended, and the Romantic dream faded into the prosaic reality of mid-nineteenth-century Europe, it was Baudelaire's mission and fate to raise his intellectual standard.

'Foie Gras to the Sound of Trumpets...'

An entertaining anthology, published over thirty years ago, was devoted to the ultimate, or penultimate, speeches of distinguished men and women. Here was the poet calling for more light; the famous statesman demanding a pork pie; Samuel Johnson meditating upon the uses of a fresh pillow or reflecting, with a certain surprise, that we shall receive no letters in the next world; the miserable author of the *Liber Amoris* observing that, after all, his career might be accounted happy. But, so far as I can recollect, one particularly illuminating remark did not find a place in the volume. Asked during his last days whether he had passed a tolerable night, 'Oh, horrid, horrid, my dear fellow!' replied Sydney Smith. 'I dreamt I was chained to a rock and being talked to death by Harriet Martineau and Macaulay.'

The joke was characteristic – not only of the speaker's humour but of his general turn of mind. He had lived to participate in the Victorian age and witness the emergence of a new society – death did not finally overtake him until 22 February 1845. But Sydney Smith, who had entered the world on 3 June 1771, never quite accommodated himself to the moral tempo of Victorian England. Hence his choice of the demons that had haunted his dreams – an indefatigable female controversialist, dedicated to the improvement of mankind, and an immensely erudite and garrulous historian, of whom Sydney Smith had already declared that, beside overflowing with learning, he was inclined to dabble in the slop. Smith was essentially a moderate man, though some of the reforms he proposed struck his contemporaries as radical, and neither paraded his learning nor flaunted his desire to do good. He was zealous and energetic; but he distrusted enthusiasm. No aristocrat himself – when he purchased a second-hand seal, he explained that hitherto the Smith family had used their thumbprints – both by temperament ánd by adoption he belonged to the society of the aristocratic Whigs, who exercised so profound an influence on English political and social life between the outbreak of the French Revolution and the passing of the First Reform Bill.

Yet, at every stage, he remained extraordinarily independent. The country clergyman who, before entering the drawing-room of a great London house, was not ashamed to change his shoes in the hall, never accepted the status of a mere parsonic pensioner, but continued to make his own rules and boldly propagate his own opinions. Few pamphleteers have been more successful; few talkers have commanded a more admiring audience. His campaign for Catholic emancipation, conducted through the celebrated series of *Peter Plymley's Letters*, combined an invocation of the spirit of Justice with an appeal to humdrum common sense. Such was his treatment of many other questions. He was at no time one of those embittered reformers whose fund of savage indignation eventually turns to self-hatred, but a sensible man – a man of the world – anxious to leave the world a less inhospitable place than he had found it. The crusades that he launched were always inspired by direct experience – against the English public school system, because he and his brother Courtenay had suffered terribly at Winchester; against the oppressive Game Laws (despite his aristocratic friends) because, as a country parson, he knew something of the hardships of the cottager's life; against militarists and warmongering politicians, because he loved peace and was deeply appreciative of the *douceur de vivre*.

For twenty-five industrious years he vented his opinions, and sometimes aired his personal prejudices, in the columns of the *Edinburgh Review*. But it was not his considerable achievement as pamphleteer and journalist that earned him the tremendous reputation he enjoyed in middle age. Although his writings had certainly prepared the ground, it was his personal character that completed the triumph. He possessed charm in an astonishing degree. Only two men are on record as having resented and disliked him – Byron who found him excessively noisy, considering that he was 'but a parson', and the Prince Regent who, in a spasm of humbug, denounced him as a 'profligate priest'. He was that very rare thing – a renowned wit whose witticisms have stood the test of time. In his conversation, as in Oscar Wilde's, there seems to have been a strong admixture of imaginative fantasy. He would take hold of a theme, decorate, enlarge it, build it up while he talked into a complex and fantastic edifice. One of his briefer excursions, for example, concerned the literary activities of Samuel Rogers. The poetaster, he said, was not very well. What was the matter? enquired a friend:

Oh, don't you know he has produced a couplet? When he is delivered of a couplet, with infinite labour and pain, he takes to his bed, has straw laid down, the knocker tied up, expects his friends to call and make enquiries, and the answer at the door invariably is 'Mr. Rogers and his little couplet are as well as can be expected.' When he produces an alexandrine he keeps his bed a day longer.

Much of his success evidently depended on discovering the right comparison, as in his well-known picture of the sloth (thrown off during the course of an article on Waterton's popular travel-book), who 'moves suspended, rests suspended, sleeps suspended, and passes his life in suspense – like a young clergyman distantly related to a bishop.' Nor was his gift of words inhibited by Victorian prudery. Some of his jokes recall Jonathan Swift, as when, in *Peter Plymley's Letters*, he suggested that the French should be brought to reason by cutting off their supply of purgatives, and described the dreadful consequences that must ensue if the bowels of mankind were occluded throughout the length and breadth of hostile Europe.

If the occasion prompted, he did not hesitate to throw in a sexual pleasantry. Agar Ellis, he wrote to Lady Holland, was vexed that he had failed to produce an heir: 'I did not say so – but I thought how absurd to discontinue the use of domestic chaplains where landed property is concerned.'

Much of the talker's abundant charm found its way into his correspondence; and his *Selected Letters*[1], is a book that deserves to be in every library and on the table beside every bed. It is full of shrewd observations and memorable phrases, and contains, incidentally, some prophetic glimpses of the future. A priest of strikingly advanced views – indeed, only a Christian in the widest and least dogmatic sense – he foresaw the gradual decline of the Church of England and the advent of a period when 'the whole act of going to church – how the Squire's Lady put on her best hat and cloak, and how the Squire bowed to the parson after church and how the parson dined with the Squire, and all these ceremonies of worship will be in the hands of the antiquarian, will be elucidated by laborious investigation, and explained by appropriate drawings.' Himself he worked hard in his parish; but he was too honest not to welcome a chance of plunging into London life, where he could exercise his great talents as a fashionable preacher and diner-out. The poets, he said, wished mankind to believe 'that happiness consists in falling in love, and living in the country – I say: live in London; like many people, fall in love with nobody.' London was his heaven on earth. As for a heaven beyond the skies, he was prepared to concede that it might perhaps exist; and, supposing that it existed, no one would be better pleased. But he had his own ideas of celestial comfort. As the reward of a long and useful career, he hoped that he might spend eternity 'eating pâtés de foie gras to the sound of trumpets'.

[1] Edited by Nowell C. Smith (ed.) *Selected Letters of Sydney Smith*, The World Classics, 1956.

A Literary Exile

The English are proud of their language; but they do not regard it as a national sanctuary, with an innermost shrine that only a true-born Englishman can ever hope to penetrate. The French, on the other hand, have a jealous and possessive affection for the tongue they have inherited; very few foreigners, according to their view, learn to speak the language either idiomatically or correctly; and still fewer manage to write it in a style that satisfies a native ear. But a single exception is admitted to prove the rule; even Sainte-Beuve readily agreed that one Englishman had composed a French masterpiece, and that he had done so, moreover, during the classic period of French prose.

To make this exception doubly surprising, the author selected was not a professional writer, but a soldier and man of the world at a loose end, who took to writing for his own diversion, and in the hope of diverting friends who had a similar background and equally mundane tastes. His opening lines set forth his intentions:

Comme ceux qui ne lisent que pour se divertir me paroissent plus raisonnables que ceux qui n'ouvrent un livre que pour y chercher des défauts, je déclare, que sans me mettre en peine de la sévère érudition de ces derniers, je n'écris que pour l'amusement des autres. Je déclare, de plus, que l'ordre des temps, ou la disposition des faits ... ne m'embarrasseront guère dans l'arrangement de ces Mémoires.

Anthony Hamilton, when he published his famous book, had nearly reached his seventieth birthday. He had been born in Ireland about 1645; and he and his five brothers – descended from an ancient Catholic family related to the Dukes of Hamilton – had seen service, under several monarchs, in many different parts of Europe. Anthony himself had fought for Louis xiv against the Dutch, and for James ii at the Battle of the Boyne. The Hamilton brothers – good-looking, debonair and gallant – seem to have had a somewhat poor opinion of that ineffective and unattractive sovereign; but (as Mademoiselle Engel remarks in her edition of the *Mémoires*[1]) they 'remained imperturbably faithful to the King whom they despised'; and after his flight from the English throne, the survivors – three of them had already been killed – followed their master into exile.

This was Anthony's second experience of exile; and, as a middle-aged man, he found it particularly irksome. The court at Saint-Germain was dull and overcrowded; Louis xiv took offence at the pride and haughtiness of the arrogant Hamilton clan; the English refugees had little money to spare, and Anthony fell back on the consolations of desultory scribbling. In order to get through his days of 'useless leisure' and keep at bay a 'boundless ennui', he began to produce not only facetious occasional verses but a series of charming fairy-stories in prose. Finally, he decided he would draw a detailed picture of the court of Charles ii, at which he himself had been presented as an elegant youth of seventeen. But the narrative evidently required a hero; and the hero he chose was his amorous and adventurous brother-in-law, Philibert de Gramont, one-time lover of Marion Delorme, who had crowned his brilliant career by capturing Elizabeth Hamilton.

Madame de Gramont, during her Whitehall apprenticeship, had been celebrated both for her beauty and for her virtue, and was said to have been one of the Maids of Honour who had had the resolution to refuse the King's advances. Their union appears to have turned out happily; and, when Gramont was believed to be dying at Fontainebleau in the year 1696, we learn that his English wife (who was suspected of

[1] *Mémoires du Chevalier de Gramont: Texte établi, annoté et présenté par Claire-Eliane Engel*, Editions du Rocher, Monaco 1958.

Jansenist tendencies) recited the Lord's Prayer at the foot of the invalid's bed. Gramont was touched and impressed. '*Cette prière est belle, comtesse,*' he observed. '*De qui est elle?*'; and, under its soothing influence, he soon recovered. Gramont survived until January, 1707 – Anthony Hamilton's *Mémoires* were published in 1713 – and Madame des Ursins, writing to Madame de Maintenon, paid a tribute to his odd and original character: '*Je ne pense pas qu'il y ait courtisan assez téméraire pour oser remplacer M. le Comte de Gramont; c'était un original qu'on ne peut imiter; sa mort n'a pas démenti sa vie.*' Apparently he had not expected death. '*Il n'y a que les sots qui meurent,*' he had once announced with his customary cynical bravado.

No doubt Hamilton had a double motive for building his story around the Comte de Gramont; he had admired, and been amused by, his personality, and saw that there would be an additional advantage in describing the English court from the standpoint of a foreign visitor. Whitehall was less magnificent than Versailles; Charles II, with his easy, natural ways, a great deal less imposing and alarming than the terrific Sun King. But then, English court-life had a gaiety and informality seldom to be enjoyed in courts across the Channel; and Hamilton emphasizes the Englishness of his subject by focusing his narrative upon a French hero and translating the chronicle of his adventures into the hero's own language. The result was a book that is neither French nor English, but has some of the distinctive qualities of both races – an admirable piece of French prose, informed by an entirely English sense of humour.

That sense of humour does not yet show signs of dating. It would be difficult to improve, for example, as an essay in literary low comedy, on Hamilton's account of how Killigrew and Rochester manage to persuade Miss Temple – '*simple, glorieuse, crédule, soupçonneuse, coquette, sage, fort suffisantè et forte sotte*' – that a forbidding maiden lady named Miss Hobart, who has warned her to beware of Lord Rochester's seductive speeches, is only playing the part of the prudent, well-meaning friend because she herself has formed horrid designs against Miss Temple's virtue; and how Miss Temple, next time her respectable friend throws an innocent arm around her waist, imagines that she is in the clutches of a she-satyr and rouses the palace with her desperate cries for help.

Hamilton's gift of lively characterization has no exact equivalent in contemporary English literature, and sometimes recalls the methods employed by a twentieth-century novelist. Thus Miss Wells, we are told, was a handsome and graceful girl; but her face, '*fait comme ceux qui plaisent le plus, était un de ceux qui plaisent le moins. Le ciel y avait répandu un certain air d'incertitude, qui lui donnait l'air d'un mouton qui rêve.*' The dreamy sheep was a devoted Royalist; '*et, comme son père avait fidèlement servi Charles I, elle crut qu'il ne fallait pas se révolter contre Charles II.*' At least, the defence she put up was exceedingly half-hearted.

Despite its frequently scandalous contents, however, which since 1817 have earned it a place on the *Index Librorum Prohibitorum*, the *Mémoires du Chevalier de Gramont* cannot be dismissed as a mere fashionable *chronique scandaleuse*. It is written in a beautifully lucid style to which no English translation can quite do justice; and, besides designing a series of memorable portraits, Hamilton shows himself a minor master of the art of story-telling. None of his portrait-sketches fails to come to life; and Hamilton's levity is sometimes as trenchant in its effect as the duc de Saint-Simon's cold severity. It would be interesting to know if he ever talked with Saint-Simon (who, although he wrote a savage obituary of Gramont, only mentions the Hamilton brothers in passing); but we are told that he was a friend of Boileau and Bussy-Rabutin, author of the *Histoire Amoureuse des Gaules*, and used to attend the literary parties held by the duchesse du Maine at Sceaux. Amid such surroundings he began to prepare the book that almost immediately established his reputation, and which was first translated into English a year after it appeared in French. Byron, we know, was devoted to the *Mémoires*, but remarked that he had never known 'a woman who did *not* protect *Rousseau*, nor one who did not dislike de Gramont. . . .' The fact was that women hated 'everything which strips off the tinsel of *Sentiment*' from the idea of human love and lust. His own *Don Juan* they disliked for the same reason. Both he and Gramont, in an age of sentiment and chivalry, had dared to tell the comic truth.

La Rochefoucauld

❧

The Fronde is a period of French history that has few attractions for the English reader, a wearisome story of intrigue and violence, made more bewildering by the vagueness of the issues at stake and by the frequency and cynical rapidity with which many of the protagonists changed sides. Yet the civil wars that kept France in a constant turmoil from 1648 to 1653 had one important literary result. They helped to produce a famous moralist, of whose masterpiece Voltaire declared that no other book had had a greater influence upon the formation of a people's taste. Having begun life as a headstrong soldier, the dashing prince de Marsillac, whose exploits included a fantastic attempt not only to rescue the Queen from her husband but to carry off at the same moment a court lady whom the King loved, he emerged at the end of the struggle, under a new title, with a new character – the disenchanted duc de La Rochefoucauld, scarred and weary both in body and in mind, a political exile, banished to a remote estate where, like many other distinguished exiles, he began to write his memoirs.

Behind him lay the life of the court and the camp; and, when he had completed his autobiography and at length returned to Paris in the year 1659, its ill-timed and unauthorized publication seriously offended the youthful Louis XIV. There could be no further hope of securing royal favour; and La Rochefoucauld, now middle-aged, was obliged to fall back on the mild amusements of a studious private life. His conduct in the Fronde had been 'detestable' – so, at least, Sainte-Beuve informs us; while his contemporary, the Cardinal de Retz, remarks that there was a mysterious *'je ne sais quoi'*, a hint of ambiguity and irresolution, about his personal character that prevented him from quite succeeding in any active rôle that he ever attempted. Somehow his boldest designs had always miscarried. He was too clear-headed – possibly too cold-hearted – to play the part of a romantic hero.

Yet popular novels remained his favourite reading; some traces of his youthful romanticism survived the disillusionments of middle life; and it was a romantic *manqué* who produced the momentous little volume of *Réflexions, Sentences et Maximes Morales* that appeared in 1665. Here La Rochefoucauld stands forth as the devil's advocate. His was an age of intense religious feeling, of gallantry and chivalric sentiment, of grandeur and heroic panache. La Rochefoucauld, in his cold, clear voice, dares to question almost every accepted ideal. He is not irreligious: *'Les Maximes de La Rochefoucauld* (writes Sainte-Beuve) *ne contredisent en rien le Christianisme, bien qu'elles s'en passent.... L'homme de La Rochefoucauld est exactement l'homme déchu....'*

He is merely the unregenerate man for whom the consolations of faith do not exist, who sees Man as the centre of the universe, but as a weak, unstable and ill-balanced centre, the victim of countless irrational beliefs and sentimental prejudices. Mankind has a high opinion of love, fostered by the poets and novelists; and La Rochefoucauld contributes his own view – he was on the eve of his long *liaison* with the exquisite Madame de La Fayette: *'Il est difficile de définir l'amour: ce qu'on en peut dire est que, dans l'âme, c'est une passion de régner; dans les esprits, c'est une sympathie; et, dans le corps, ce n'est qu'une envie cachée et délicate de posséder ce que l'on aime, après beaucoup de mystères.'* But he hastens to add that what we usually mistake for love is very often pure invention. Talk of true love recalls our talk about ghosts. Everybody tells ghost stories; not many of us can claim to have encountered a spectre. Human beings tend to fall in love because they imagine that they ought to fall in love: '*Il y a des gens qui n'auraient jamais été amoureux, s'ils n'avaient jamais entendu parler de l'amour.*'

In a similar spirit, he deals with friendship and marriage, with female chastity and worldly ambition and the supposed advantages of a courtier's existence. To self-interest he traces the great majority of human feelings, and to self-delusion most of the joys that appear to make our life worth living. How much is left? Perhaps only a sense of style and the knowledge that one possesses a fund of inward strength. There is also a somewhat mournful comfort in knowing that one is not deceived, in studying the world as it is rather than as we would have it be. La Rochefoucauld's pessimistic vision takes him far into the realms of psychology; and on the subject of passion and sexual jealousy he occasionally anticipates the ideas of Proust: '*Plus on aime une maîtresse* (he announces) *plus on est près de la hair.*' But jealousy sometimes outlives passion: '*La jalousie nait toujours avec l'amour; mais elle ne meurt pas toujours avec lui.*' A capacity for suffering may prove to be very much more durable than the pleasures from which that suffering sprang.

That we should banish self-deception and eschew humbug are the only moral remedies that La Rochefoucauld offers. Let us on no account pretend to be more sensitive than we really are or indulge in a parade of fine feelings: '*Nous avons tous assez de force pour supporter les maux d'autrui.*' The gifted and warm-hearted Madame de La Fayette is said to have persuaded her lover to tone down certain of his sternest maxims; but naturally, both in France and abroad, they have made him many fierce enemies. Rousseau regarded his book as highly pernicious; Voltaire, on the other hand, praised it and delighted in it. La Rochefoucauld, he says, accustomed the civilized writer '*à penser et à renfermer ses pensées dans un tour vif, précis et délicat; c'était un mérite que personne n'avait eu avant lui, en Europe, depuis la renaissance de lettres.*' No translation can quite catch the tone of his voice – cynical without acrimony, reserved and often melancholic, but without a hint of self-pity. La Rochefoucauld lived on into the *Grand Siècle* and, at length forgiven for his youthful escapades, was accepted as an interesting and picturesque survivor at the court of Louis XIV, dying in 1680 at the age of sixty-six. Madame de Sévigné lamented his passing, and Bossuet visited his sickroom to administer the last rites.

The Magician of Pleasure

Our anxious septuagenarian century was once a period of hope and promise. Difficult to believe, perhaps. It is none the less true that, for many young French writers and painters who began their creative existence about the year 1900, the shadows of a bad old world seemed to be fading away, while radiant prospects shone ahead. These latter-day enthusiasts breathed much the same exhilarating atmosphere as had been breathed by the young Wordsworth and his friends; but the revolution that inspired them was scientific and mechanical rather than political: 'We should love our own times', cried Guillaume Apollinaire. '... We are living in a marvellous age, full of burning imagination and fascinating progress.' Science, felt Apollinaire and his band of associates, had dealt a death-stroke to 'the past we no longer love', and had thrown open gigantic territories for the creative artist to explore at leisure. They prophesied 'a profound renewal ... of societies, myths, the arts, philosophy....'

Among youthful painters, the fiery Pablo Ruiz, soon to become famous as Picasso, who had reached Paris in 1899, and who in 1907 produced his historic canvas, *Les Demoiselles d'Avignon*, already played a dashing part; while Max Jacob, who, at each new work that Picasso showed him, would exclaim provocatively 'Still too Symbolist!', was among the numerous poets and critics now mustered on the revolutionary side. As for Apollinaire, he was both a notable poet himself and the literary spokesman of the new movement. His volume devoted to *Les Peintres Cubistes* laid down the basic principles of Cubist art, which would break through the outward husk of reality to disclose a deeper reality beneath. The intentions of the Cubist leaders were nothing if not ambitious. '*L'art des peintres nouveaux,*' he wrote, '*prend l'univers infini comme idéal*'.

Apollinaire was also a gifted creator of myths; and many of the legends he spun concerned the circumstances of his private life. He was by nature – and he chose to remain – a slightly ambiguous and mysterious personage, not a Frenchman born, though French was his language and he was thoroughly acclimatized to the Gallic literary tradition. Particularly secretive about his parental origins, he managed to conceal them so adroitly that only during the last few years has it been possible to tell the whole truth. In fact, Apollinaire, christened Wilhelm Alberto Appollinario, was the illegitimate son of Angelica Kostrowitsky, the unruly daughter of a distinguished Polish exile, and of a middle-aged Italian ex-officer, Francesco Flugi d'Aspermont. The latter presently abandoned his mistress; and the raffish, exuberant Madame Kostrowitsky, whom her son admired and feared, dragged Wilhelm and her younger son round the watering places and gambling resorts of Europe. Wherever she went, she gambled desperately and almost always unsuccessfully, living under the temporary protection of a series of indulgent but ill-treated lovers.

After many awkward and humiliating vicissitudes, the family settled down in Paris; and there Wilhelm Kostrowitsky, otherwise Guillaume Apollinaire, found at length his true home. Throughout his life, his latest biographer suggests, he yearned for the sense of security that he had seldom known in childhood; he wished 'to belong', to be received and accepted; and, even as a revolutionary poet, he could never bring himself quite to break with the literary traditions of the past. Hence the peculiarity of the position he occupied: hence the highly original use that he made of his lively imagination and his fine poetic flair. He was seeking, he announced, for 'a lyricism that will be at once new and humanistic'. And on another occasion: 'God is my witness that I have only tried to add new domains to art and literature, without in any way refusing to recognize the masterpieces of the past and the present. . . .' Paul Verlaine and François Villon were masters for whom he had a special cult; and, like them, he attempted to infuse his verse with something of the spontaneous rhythm of common speech; he dislocated Romantic and Symbolist patterns – now and then with the help of eccentric typographical devices – in order to set free the living spirit of poetry.

At his best, he was an enchanting lyric poet; and as a poet he can afford to stand alone – this Italian-Pole has added his assumed name to the great chronicle of French literature. As a powerful propagandist, nevertheless, a magnetic personal influence, a brilliant intermediary between writers and painters, in those golden days when writers and painters enjoyed the same lofty hopes and seemed to speak the same language, Apollinaire also deserves the modern reader's attention. Among his associates were such painters as Picasso, Braque and Modigliani, such writers as Max Jacob, André Salmon, Blaise Cendrars and Alfred Jarry, creator of *Le Roi Ubu*, the perverse and arrogant 'Super-Male', who would perambulate the boulevards in Apollinaire's company, discoursing on art and life like a fallen archangel and occasionally terrifying bourgeois pedestrians by letting off a pistol-shot.

For his companions, Apollinaire was the 'magician of pleasure', gourmet, amorist, bohemian, man of learning, always engaged in some unexpected, and usually unhappy love affair. There are men who transform whatever they touch; and Apollinaire, the inimitable myth-maker, gave his whole existence an air of legendary strangeness. Seen through his eyes, even a London surburb becomes a wild and haunted place; and when he fell in love with a modest English girl and followed her across the Channel, the result was a characteristic sheaf of poems entitled *L'Emigrant de Landor Road*, which records his impressions of Annie's native streets, of the glaring shop-fronts and advertisements of the West end, and the dark and sinister lanes down which he had wandered near the London Docks.

Annie had numerous successors, each of whom he commemorated in literary form – the painter Marie Laurencin, who suddenly threw him over: Louise de Coligny-Chatillon, *Le P'tit Lou*, a rakish young woman of aristocratic descent, who in her turn deserted him: Madeleine Pagès, a bluestocking schoolmistress, to whom he was briefly engaged but afterwards, wisely no doubt, decided that he would not marry. In his relations with women, Apollinaire, we are told, was both sensual and romantically elusive, both the predatory 'Polish hussar' and a poetic mage exploring the secrets of the heart. By 1914 – despite an alarming and embarrassing reverse, when he was suspected of having connived at the theft of certain ancient statuettes from the Louvre and cast into a noisome Parisian gaol – his reputation, as a renowned poet and a redoubtable personality alike, was already well established; but, that summer, the declaration of war revealed him in yet another aspect. He devoted himself to a military life with all the enthusiasm that he had formerly shown as the prophet of the Cubist revolution, wrote a series of admirable war-poems, was gravely wounded and invalided out of the army, only to die, late in 1918, of an attack of Spanish influenza. He was then thirty-eight. 'Save me, Doctor, I have still so much to say,' were his last despairing words.

Taine in England

✤

A rewarding anthology might one day be compiled of traveller's tales brought home from England, reports on our manners and morals by distinguished foreign tourists who visited these always mysterious shores between the end of the Napoleonic struggle and the beginning of the twentieth century. Chateaubriand, I suppose, would head the procession, with his dramatic glimpses in *Mémoires d'outre tombe* of the two Englands he had personally inspected – before the Industrial Revolution, a garden-paradise shaped by a triumphant aristocracy according to its own design; later, a Satanic landscape of forges, furnaces and factory chimneys.

Heine, who detested England because he loved Napoleon and abominated Wellington, arrived here in the late 1820s. 'Send no poet to England!' (he warned his compatriots). 'This downright earnestness ... this colossal uniformity, this machine-like movement, this moroseness even in pleasure ... smothers the imagination and rends the heart.' But, besides famous poets, room would also be found for such entertaining oddities as Prince Pückler-Muskau, who visited us in 1814 and again in 1842, and wrote admirable descriptions of an opulent English country house and a well-appointed London club.

Another gifted student of our national *mores* was Guillaume-Sulpice Chevallier, more celebrated under his pseudonym Gavarni, who landed at Folkestone towards the close of December, 1847, and remained here for several years, sketching and observing up and down the kingdom. Like Heine and Pückler-Muskau, Gavarni was deeply impressed by the English feeling for material comfort:

*C'est le plus charmant pays du monde que cette Angleterre,
pour y vivre de la vie matérielle, mais . . . le coeur ne saurait ici
s'appuyer sur rien. C'est parce qu'ils manquent de coeur que
les Anglais sont si peu gênants. . . .*

Gavarni had studied women in an almost entomological spirit;
and he was naturally much interested in the phenomenon of
respectable Victorian womanhood:

*Quant aux Anglaises, je vous en parlerais bien, mais j'ignore
absolument ce que c'est: tout ce que j'imagine, c'est que,
lorsqu'une Anglaise est habillée, ce n'est plus une femme, c'est
une cathédrale. Il ne s'agirait pas de la séduire, mais de la
démolir. Or, je ne suis pas séducteur, – je suis aussi moins
demolisseur . . . .*

On a different plane, he was astounded and horrified by the
dark misery of the London slums, and produced a long series
of telling lithographs devoted to beggars, slum-children and
bare-footed vagrants. Paul Verlaine, towards the end of the
procession, saw very little of London's splendour – '*plat
comme une punaise qui serait noire, London!*' – but a great
deal of its proletarian squalor, as with Rimbaud he perambu-
lated the public houses of the Tottenham Court Road and
listened to the ribald back-chat of the local prostitutes –

*d'exquises miss à la longue jupe de satin groseille, jaspée de
boue, tigrée de consommes épandues, trouée de chiures de
cigarettes . . .*

Hippolyte Taine would occupy an important place in the
proposed anthology. He made three expeditions across the
Channel – in 1859, 1862 and 1871; and from each visit he
brought home a mass of notes on Anglo-Saxon life and characters. His *Notes on England*, in its translated form, is a work of
nearly 300 closely printed pages. Taine was neither an artist
nor, at least as regards England, always a very sound psychologist; but he had an inquiring mind and a philosophical outlook – '*une imagination Germanique administrée et exploitée
par une raison latine,*' one of his biographers said – and plods

146

conscientiously around his subject, studying, measuring, evaluating.

London had received him in its most forbidding mood – with one of those wet Sundays which the English Opium-Eater found so terrible. And that hideous Sabbath, when the strange metropolis presented the aspect of a 'vast, and well-kept graveyard,' was soon followed by an all-enveloping fog: 'In this livid smoke, objects are no more than phantoms and nature looks like a bad drawing in charcoal on which some-one has rubbed his sleeve.' Everywhere the fog left disfigur-ing traces; in the parks, it had even besmirched the trees. But particularly hideous were the 'colonnades, peristyles and Greek ornaments, the mouldings and garlands on the houses, all washed with soot. . . . On the façades of the British Mu-seum the flutings of the columns are full of greasy filth, as if sticky mud had been set flowing down them.'

A critic of art and a lover of beauty, Taine was astonished and appalled by the garish fashions that Victorian women affected, 'violet dresses, of a really ferocious violet, encircled at the waist by a gold belt,' purple gloves, absurd hats 'trimmed with clumps of red flowers and enormous rib-bons. . . .' The landscape itself, when he reached the country, did not strike him as entirely beautiful, though he admired the opaline transparency of its hues if the sun illuminated them through a veil of mist. But surely the grass was too green – too vivid to be quite bearable? No, the English pro-spect was not harmonious. And the same lack of harmony could be observed in the proportions of the English social structure.

Immense wealth co-existed with evidences of degraded poverty. An Englishman was considered by no means rich – merely 'comfortable' and well-established – on an income of eight thousand pounds a year. Yet, not very far from the monotonous squares and crescents where the rich and the moderately affluent lived, one stumbled on courts and lanes peopled by a dense conglomeration of proletarian Yahoos. Taine inspected the slums of London and later visited the slums of Liverpool, wandering along broken pavements and peering through decrepit doorways:

What rooms! A threadbare slip of oilcloth on the floor, sometimes a big seashell or one or two plaster ornaments. ... The children tumble over each other. The smell is that of an old-clothes shop full of rotting rags. ... As we went forward the crowds grew denser. ... Bearded old women came out of gin-shops their reeling gait, dismal eyes and fixed, idiot grin are indescribable.

The drunkenness of the slums shocked the foreign observer; and he added that in the middle class, too, the English mode of debauchery seemed painfully depressing. Vice was stripped of the smallest pretence of refinement: the gin-smelling streetwalkers of the Haymarket took the place of the elegant Parisian *lorette* and the obliging, good-tempered *grisette*. Nevertheless, Taine felt a respect for England which gradually increased as he came to know us better. Despite the pernicious effects of commercial *laissez-faire*, he appreciated the British system of government.

'On the whole [he wrote] whereas we *suffer* our government, the English *support* theirs.' Somehow or other, the English had inherited a rare capacity for co-operative effort. The poorer classes might be dressed in cast-off rags; while 'the French workman's blouse or overall is his own . . . it has been worn by nobody but himself.' Yet, strangely enough, they did not hate their superiors; and the rich, at their best, showed a sense of responsibility towards the poor. Responsibility – that was the word! There was something authoritative, dignified, self-contained about members of the upper classes: the girls in Hyde Park who sat their horses so well and, notwithstanding their ridiculous clothes, were so virginal and so seductive, and their fathers, brothers and suitors, who managed huge estates, administered local justice, served in the Brigade of Guards and sat in Parliament.

Taine was equally pleased by the English conception of family life. Domestic felicity and the relationships of parents and children (he noted) were among the themes most frequently illustrated in *Punch*. Young men aspired to marriage, instead of devoting their attention to casual affairs; and adultery was uncommon, both in middle-class and in aristocratic circles, although now and then a rich gentleman might develop an affection for a trademan's wife. 'An Englishman in a state of adultery is miserable: even at the supreme moment his conscience torments him. As for the "kept woman", she is carefully hidden. Reserve, in this matter, is obligatory and extreme.'

Taine's picture of England may be by no means complete – Victorian society was not unfamiliar with horrific matrimonial scandals; but it deserves scrutiny as the impression of an unusually intelligent and inquisitive mind. Some of his statements are exaggerated; but his book is full of small amusing touches, such as his reference to the fact that Parisian artisans, after the recent commercial treaty, sometimes refused to purchase English tools because, although they were cheap and well made, *'cela n'a pas d'oeil'*. For all their obvious merits, English saws and hammers lacked the appropriately stylish air.

Mayhew's London

❧

During the fourth and fifth centuries after Christ, the ordered landscape of the Roman world suffered a disastrous transformation. The imperial system was slowly breaking down; and, while the great landowners withdrew to remote fortified demesnes (where, if they were originally of Roman descent, they soon took on the manners and costume of outlandish barbarian neighbours), the huge open cities, which had expanded under the sun of *pax romana*, with their libraries and their baths, their market-places and their temples, shrank into smaller and meaner compass, behind massive walls often constructed from the debris of demolished shrines and palaces. Aqueducts had been breached, flooding the farm lands; as travel grew more dangerous, the post roads were neglected. Fugitives thronged into the safer townships; the mediaeval city began to appear, picturesque, squalid and overcrowded, with its girdle of crenellated ramparts, its narrow, tortuous streets, its confusion and its poverty.

For more than a thousand years, almost up to the dawn of the Industrial Revolution, most European cities belonged to the Middle Ages, both in their design and in their outlook. Many of them preserved their gates and walls; and through the gates a citizen could walk without hindrance into the unpolluted countryside. As late as the opening of the nineteenth century, Londoners, though they might grumble at the stink and congestion and noise of their immense metropolis, were never far separated from country sights and sounds. Three windmills could be viewed from the Strand; and even the most sedentary inhabitant of the thoroughfares between Oxford Street and Piccadilly had only to stroll westwards beyond Hyde Park Corner, or northwards through the fields behind Portland Place, to lose himself in some rambling lane among meadows, hawthorn-trees and market-gardens. But already the speculators were hard at work; waves of brick advanced upon farm and garden; Cockney terraces and squares and crescents sprang up with bewildering rapidity on London's urban outskirts, filling the green space between the nucleus of the city and its small surrounding villages. A new type of city was being born; a new civilization was emerging, from which would spring a potent and incalculable force in modern European literature.

Henceforward, the majority of writers, by necessity or habit, would be first and foremost city-dwellers; and urban life would give their work a very definite, at times harsh, but extremely individual colouring. They would love the city as much as they hated it. Among French writers, we think immediately of Charles Baudelaire, whose imagination was deeply stirred by the spectacle of mid-nineteenth-century Paris, in which the ancient, intimate metropolis of his boyhood was nowadays dissolving and disappearing; and, on this side of the English Channel, London was at once the nursery and the forcing-house of Charles Dickens' utterly dissimilar and completely Anglo-Saxon genius. Though it may be wrong to assert that, without London, there would have been no Dickens, it is undoubtedly true that, had he been brought up in any other city or in any other period, his novels would have lost something of their peculiar strangeness.

Eighteenth-century London was still small enough to be compact and personal; its industries were localized; the structure of its social life was relatively uncomplicated. During Dickens' lifetime, however, a tremendous influx of population bought with it a corresponding loss of freedom, health and dignity. The individual was submerged in the mass of anonymous toilers, whose whole world was circumscribed by the bricks and mortar of whatever nook or cranny they had been shoved into by circumstance. From the ranks of these little people, these waifs and oddities and misfits – human rubbish thrown up by the struggle for existence conducted on principles of economic *laissez faire* – the novelist drew the raw material of those fascinating minor personages who constitute the all-important background of any Dickens story, the creepers and the climbers, the grovellers and the schemers, scrambling over one another in the dark confusion of their pestiferous urban ant's-nest.

With every decade, their number increased. During the first thirty years of the nineteenth century, the population of the Greater London area rose from 865,000 to 1,500,000; and during the next twenty years another million inhabitants were somehow piled in. They were housed (writes a contributor to that valuable compilation, *Early Victorian England*) 'by overcrowding, and by lateral expansion in houses, mainly two-storied, built on estates it was desired to develop, and ribboned along roads. That is why, in the *Pickwick Papers,* Mr Wicks, of Dodson and Fogg's, found it was "half past four before he got to Somers Town" after a convivial evening . . . and Mr Jaggers cultivated the family affections behind a ditch in Walworth.' As the populace thickened, so did its occupations grow more miscellaneous, its character more and more amorphous. Parasites fastened on parasites; the refuse and leavings of one class helped, literally as well as figuratively, to provide a means of livelihood for the class immediately beneath it; and, while the poor but 'respectable' members of commercial society, the clerks and small employees, tended to gravitate towards pretentious gimcrack suburbs which had pullulated upon London's shabby outer edge, the lowest and weakest of its citizens, the scavengers, rag-pickers and pedlars, drifted into its noisome central slums, into one or other of the many 'rookeries', clusters of dilapidated ancient houses, such as 'Tom All Alone's,' under the shadow of Westminster Abbey, scathingly described in *Bleak House*.

The first chapters of that novel – together with *Our Mutual Friend*, probably Dickens' most ambitious attempt to delineate the London Landscape – were published in periodical form during the spring of 1852. But the public conscience was already aroused; for the Victorian age was neither self-complacent nor insensitive; and throughout the 1830s and 1840s repeated plans had been made for the delivery of at least a preliminary attack on the gigantic Augean stable that London, at its then rate of development, was in danger of becoming. There were sanitary commissions, inquests on water-supply; and a vast and compendious *Report on the Sanitary Condition of the City of London* for the years 1848–49 provoked the indignation and excited the alarm of every thoughtful Londoner. Though 'rookeries' still bred disease, their existence was threatened, if not by the moral scruples of the English ruling classes, at all events by the practical necessity of opening up new thoroughfares; and, to clear the approaches to New London Bridge, a million and a half pounds' worth of old property had been purchased and demolished. The spirit of reform and philanthropy was omnipresent; and, by a singular stroke of good fortune, an enterprising philanthropist of the period happened, at the same time, to be an extremely able journalist. Two volumes of articles, which had originally appeared in the London daily press, were collected by their author, Henry Mayhew, and published, under the title *London Labour & the London Poor*, in 1851.

On the career of this gifted and industrious man the *Dictionary of National Biography* is concise and informative, but somewhat unenthusiastic. Born in 1812, the son of a London attorney, he survived till 1887. His activities during that time were numerous and varied. He began his working life as a dramatist, his first production being a one-act play entitled 'The Wandering Minstrel' in which he introduced the celebrated Cockney song, 'Villikins and his Dinah', and was the author of many other successful comedies and farces. As a middle-aged journalist, he attended at the birth of *Punch*, of which for a while he acted as joint editor; and, in addition to his dramatic, journalistic and philanthropic efforts, he found time to turn out travel-books, biographies, novels and stories and treatises on popular science. The bulk of his work was ephemeral; but there can be no doubt that *London Labour & the London Poor*, reissued in 1861, 1862, 1864 and 1865 with copious additions and supplementary volumes, is an achievement that deserves the respectful attention of posterity. Not only was Mayhew a pioneer in this particular type of sociological record; but, thanks to the original cast of his mind and to his extraordinary gifts both as an observer and as a reporter, he left behind him a book that one need not be a student of history or a sociologist to find immensely entertaining.

The plan is ambitious. Disregarding the strongholds of wealth and privilege, Mayhew set out to plumb the dark ocean of poverty or semi-poverty by which they were encircled, to discover how the poor lived – the hopelessly poor, as well as the depressed and struggling – and to examine the means, ignoble and commendable, furtive and above-board, by which the majority of London's unorganized millions precariously scraped a livelihood. Had he been exclusively concerned with economics, Mayhew's *magnum opus* might make useful but tedious reading. In fact, his interests were many-sided; and no less than three persons appear and re-appear as we turn the pages of his survey. First, there is the impassioned Statistician; but here, it must be admitted, Mayhew with the best intentions in the world is often slightly absurd. He loved figures for their own sake, and welcomed every opportunity of drawing up vast ingenious tables. Thus, when he considered the problem of street-cleaning and street-cleaners, besides classifying the sweepers themselves, analysing their economic position and depicting their personal habits, he produced a catalogue, entitled *Food Consumed By and Excretions of a Horse in Twenty-Four Hours*.

Nor is the catalogue allowed to speak for itself. Mayhew follows it up with the results of an investigation into the metabolic processes of a 'Brown horse of middle size', conducted at the Royal Veterinary College on September 29th, 1849, and goes on to discuss the trouble caused to London street-cleaners by the passage through the streets of cattle, calves, sheep and pigs. Luckily, another aspect of Mayhew's personality is very soon in evidence. As the philanthropic Social Investigator, he feels a deep concern with the material needs and financial vicissitudes of his fellow human beings. He is intensely preoccupied with the lives of others; and no detail is so trifling that it can slip through the meshes of his inquisitorial drag-net. We are informed, for example, that a working scavenger of the 1850s, having earned fifteen shillings by his week's labour, had spent, in the instance selected, the sum of exactly thirteen shillings and twopence-farthing – one-and-ninepence being the rent of an unfurnished room, sevenpence going on tobacco, two-and-fourpence on beer, one-and-a-penny on gin, a penny-three-farthings on pickles or onions, and two-and-fourpence on boiled salt beef. A journeyman sweeper was maintained by his master at the cost of approximately sixpence-halfpenny. But 'on Sundays the fare was better. They then sometimes had a bit of "prime fat mutton taken to the oven, with 'taturs to bake along with it". or a "fry of liver, if the 'oman was in a good humour", and always a pint of beer apiece.' But Londoners had not only to be fed; they must also be clothed; and in certain callings a decent appearance must be carefully kept up:

'A prosperous and respectable master green-grocer (writes Mayhew), who was that may be called "particular" in his dress, as he had been a gentleman's servant, and was now in the habit of waiting upon the wealthy persons in his neighbourhood, told me that the following was the average of his washing bill. He was a bachelor; all his washing was put out;

	s.	d.
Two shirts (per week)	0	7
Stockings	0	1
Night-shirt (worn two weeks generally, average per week)	0	¾
Sheets, blankets, and other household linens or woollens	0	2
Handkerchiefs	0	¼
	0	11

and he considered his expenditure far *above* the average of his class, as many used no nightshirt, but slept in the shirt they wore during the day, and paid only 3d., and even less, per shirt to their washer-woman, and perhaps, and more especially in winter, made one shirt last the week.

These details may serve to illustrate the meticulous humanity with which Mayhew pursued his subject. And now a further facet of his character emerges. It would be presumptuous, no doubt, to call him the nineteenth-century Defoe; but, if he had none of Defoe's imaginative genius, he had the same devotion to the literal fact, the same grasp of detail and the same observant eye, that makes Defoe the most poetic of the great European realists. Mayhew's notes on economic conditions were accompanied by brilliant portraits of individual men and women. One would like to know what were his methods of work. This Victorian mass-observer would appear to have spent long hours of conversation in attics, public houses and back-streets, asking innumerable questions and patiently noting down the answers. Here he reveals his third facet – perhaps the most important – the dispassionate Literary Portraitist, who bore some resemblance both to Daniel Defoe and to Restif de la Bretonne.

Like them he browsed and botanized; but he had a knack of recording living speech that was peculiarly characteristic of the period he lived in. Take, for instance, this speech by an old soldier:

I'm 42 now (he said), and when I was a boy and a young man I was employed in the *Times* machine office, but got into a bit of a row—a bit of a street quarrel and frolic, and was called on to pay £3, something about a street-lamp; that was out of the question; and as I was taking a walk in the park, not just knowing what I'd best do, I met a recruiting sergeant, and enlisted on a sudden—all on a sudden—in the 16th Lancers. ...Well, I was rather frolicsome in those days, I confess, and perhaps *had rather a turn for a roving life*, so when the sergeant said he'd take me to the East India Company's recruiting sergeant, I consented, and was accepted at once. I was taken to Calcutta, and served under General Nott all through the Afghan war. The first real warm work I was in was at Candahar. I've heard young soldiers say that they've gone into action the first time as merry as they would go to a play. Don't believe them, Sir. Old soldiers will tell you quite different. You *must* feel queer and serious the first time you're in action; it's not fear—it's nervousness. The crack of the muskets at the first fire you hear in real hard earnest is uncommon startling; you see the flash of the fire from the enemy's line, but very little else. Indeed, oft enough you see nothing but smoke, and hear nothing but balls whistling every side of you. And then you get excited, just as if you were at a hunt; but after a little service—I can speak for myself, at any rate—you go into action as you go to your dinner.

'Something about a street-lamp'—how admirable the phrase is! Mayhew's pages are illuminated, again and again, by these sudden vivid flashes in which the essentials of a situation or character—here the headstrong young man on a spree; the tinkle of broken glass; the mood of exhilaration passing into the mood of angry desperation during which he meets the sergeant—seem concisely summed up. As memorable are his impressions of interiors; for his omnivorous curiosity was not confined to street-life; and, bound on a visit to an impoverished costermonger, he had climbed a flight of tottering and broken stairs, and entered a room thick with the smoke that was pouring from the chimney:

The place was filled with it, curling in the light, and making everything so indistinct that I could with difficulty see the white mugs ranged in the corner-cupboard. ... On a mattress, on the floor, lay a pale-faced girl—'eighteen years old last twelfth-cake day'—her drawn-up form showing in the patch-work counterpane that covered her. She had just been confined, and the child had died! ... To shield her from the light of the window, a cloak had been fastened up slantingly across the panes; and on a string that ran along the wall was tied, amongst the bonnets, a clean nightcap—'against the doctor came', as the mother, curtsying, informed me .... The room was about nine feet square, and furnished a home for three women. The ceiling slanted like that of a garret, and was the colour of old leather, excepting a few rough white patches, where the tenants had rudely mended it. The daylight was easily seen through the laths, and in one corner a large patch of the paper looped down from the wall. . . . They had made a carpet out of three or four old mats. They were 'obligated to it for fear of dropping anything through the boards into the donkey stables in the parlour underneath. But we only pay ninepence a week rent,' said the old woman, 'and mustn't grumble'.

Mayhew's impressions, however, are not of gloom unmitigated or poverty unrelieved; and many have the cheerfulness and distinction of a Dutch or Flemish *genre* picture. He describes, for example, his visit to the home of a thriving coster-monger, where 'the floor was as white as if it had been newly planed', and 'the wall over the fire-place was patched up to the ceiling with little square pictures of saints. . . . On the mantel-piece, between a row of bright tumblers and wine glasses filled with odds and ends, stood glazed crockeryware images of Prince Albert and M. Jullien. . . . In the band-box, which stood on the stained chest of drawers, you could tell that the Sunday bonnet was stowed away safely from the dust.'

Even the room occupied by a family of struggling costers was not entirely squalid:

The man, a tall, thick-built, almost good-looking fellow, with a large fur cap on his head, lived with his family in a front kitchen, and as there were, with his mother-in-law, five persons and only one bed, I was somewhat puzzled to know where they could *all* sleep. The barrow standing on the railings over the window, half shut out the light, and when any one passed there was a momentary shadow thrown over the room, and a loud rattling of the iron gratings above that completely prevented all conversation. When I entered, the mother-in-law was reading aloud one of the threepenny papers to her son, who lolled on the bed, that with its curtains nearly filled the room. There was the usual attempt to make the fireside comfortable. The stone sides had been well whitened, and the mantel-piece decorated with its small tin trays, tumblers, and a piece of looking-glass. A cat with her kittens were seated on the hearth-rug in front. . . . By the drawers were piled up four bushel baskets, and in a dark corner near the bed stood a tall measure full of apples that scented the room. .... On a string dangled a couple of newly washed shirts, and by the window were two stone barrels, for lemonade, when the coster visited the fairs and races.

Still more vivid, in its extremely Dickensian way, is Mayhew's account of his meeting with Jack Black, 'Rat and mole destroyer to Her Majesty', whom he discovered at his house in Battersea, and whose expression radiated a kindliness that did not 'exactly agree with one's preconceived notions of rat-catchers. His face had a strange appearance, from his rough, uncombed hair being nearly grey, and his eyebrows and whiskers black, so that he looked as if he wore powder'. He, too, lived surrounded by the apparatus of his daily work – he was, incidentally, taxidermist and bird-fancier as well as rat-catcher; his parlour was 'more like a shop than a family apartment. In a box ... like a rabbit-hutch, was a white ferret, twisting its long thin body with a snake-like motion, up and down the length of its prison, as restlessly as if it were a miniature polar bear. When Mr Black called "Polly" to the ferret, it came to the bars and fixed its pink eyes on him. A child lying on the floor poked its fingers into the cage, but Polly only smelt at them. . . .'

Nothing is more remarkable about Mayhew's book than the fantastic diversity of trades and occupations that came beneath his survey. Besides street-sellers innumerable, vending every kind of object from nutmeg-graters and tracts to dogs and birds-nests, there were (in addition to sweepers and scavengers) a considerable class of 'finders' who existed, from hand to mouth, on the material they picked up. In the first class – the itinerant street-merchants – the London coster-mongers were probably the most vigorous and independent. They had their own dress, which Mayhew describes at length, their own public-houses and slang and round of social gaieties; they patronized 'the Vic Gallery', frequented 'two-penny hops', were fond of gambling, singing, fighting but, in spite of their brutal and pugnacious habits, were devoted to their donkeys. Such were the chivalry of London back-streets. On a lower level – physically and morally, if not always financially – was the section of the populace that dealt in London's ordures.

This section was sharply subdivided. At one end of the scale were 'mud-larks' and 'pure-finders', the poorest of the poor, destitute children or aged men and women, some of whom, like the 'mud-larks', gathered lumps of coal or fragments of old iron from London's slimy riverside, where they spent their days wading and grubbing among the refuse of the mud-banks; while others – the 'pure-finders – scoured the pavements for the droppings of dogs, which they then sold by the pailfull to some local tannery. Their earnings were as meagre. But this branch of commerce had its aristocracy; and Mayhew devotes one of his most curious and entertaining chapters to the 'toshers' or sewer-hunters, whose business it was, before the building of the Thames embankment, to explore the urban sewer-system which still opened on the fore-shore.

Their work was profitable but uncommonly dangerous. London's sewers during the 1850s were ancient, dilapidated and of unknown extent. Some dated from the Middle Ages; the brickwork at any moment might collapse on the ex-plorer's head; he might be stifled by sewer-gas; hordes of fero-cious sewer-rats might attack and overwhelm him, and, be-fore help came, pick his bones clean; or he might be drowned by an unusually high tide gurgling up unperceived through the labyrinthine passages of his mephitic underworld. But on the proceeds of what they discovered – old iron, copper coins, even sovereigns and silver tea-spoons – the toshers could ex-pect to clear a far bigger profit than often came the way of the ordinary industrious above-ground London artisan. Nor did their health suffer. Though it was a 'roughish smell at first' (as one of them admitted), the atmosphere of the sewers soon ceased to incommode them; and the 'toshers', as a class, were 'strong, robust, and healthy men, generally florid in their complexion'. Their personal habits were regrettably intemperate. '... Like all who make a living as it were by a game of chance, plodding carefulness, and saving habits cannot be reckoned among their virtues. . . . The shoremen might, with but ordinary prudence, live well, have comfortable homes, and even be able to save sufficient to provide for themselves in their old age. Their practice, however, is directly the reverse. They no sooner make a 'haul', as they say, than they adjourn to some low public house in the neighbourhood, and seldom leave till empty pockets and hungry stomachs drive them forth to procure the means of a fresh debauch. 'It is principally on this account (writes Mayhew) that, despite their large gains, they are to be found located in the most wretched quarter of the metropolis' – for example, in a court off Rosemary Lane, entered 'through a dark narrow entrance . . . running beneath the first floor of one of the houses in the adjoining street, and surrounded by tall wooden tenements, with overhanging upper storeys. The court was densely populated; and every room contained its own family.' But few of the inhabitants employed their proper names; it was as 'Lanky Bill', 'Long Tim', One-eyed George', 'Short-armed Jack' that they were known to all their neighbours.

Evelyn Waugh

My first meeting with Evelyn Waugh must have occurred well over forty years ago, some time early in the 1920s, when I was living at home in the small Hertfordshire town of Berkhamsted, and attending the local grammar school, where Graham Greene's father, Charles Greene – Graham himself attended the school – was established as the headmaster.

Several successful writers inhabited Berkhamsted, among them the celebrated Victorian storyteller, W. W. Jacobs, a renowned professional humorist with one of the most lugubrious faces I have ever seen. I knew his family and often visited his house; and I was presently excited to learn that his eldest daughter had just become engaged to the daring young rebel Alex Waugh, author of that highly controversial novel *The Loom of Youth*. Alec soon appeared in Berkhamsted, looking as cheerful and rubicund as he does today; and he was quickly followed by his brother Evelyn, a slight, curly-headed, dandified figure wearing a coloured waistcoat and carrying, I seem to remember, a pair of lemon-yellow gloves.

Some years later, when I arrived in Oxford, Evelyn Waugh, still slender, alert and dandified, came round to Balliol to call on me. The novelist's future biographers – no doubt he will have more than one – should pay special attention to the varying circumstances of his youth and early manhood. Between the time he left Oxford and the moment he emerged as a rising literary artist, he managed – how or for what reasons a critic can only guess – almost completely to transform his character.

The juvenile Waugh had been carefree, gay and affectionate

– though in his cups he sometimes revealed a strain of anarchic desperation. The adult Waugh was sombre and cross-grained, and treated most of his fellow human beings as villains, cranks or pestilential boobies. His co-religionists found him warm-hearted; I am told that he frequently did good by stealth. But to doubt his beliefs or question his prejudices was immediately to be thrust outside the pale. Nobody was so fond of drawing a line; and the lines that Evelyn drew gradually cut him off – much, it must be conceded, to his own satisfaction – from nine-tenths of the modern world.

His Oxford period itself fell into two separate phases. During the opening phase he occupied airy and agreeable rooms, where he was surrounded by his drawings and woodcuts – he was then an industrious amateur draughtsman – and by the Nonesuch editions of the English classics. Then he experienced a sudden reverse, sold most of his books and objects of art at an uproarious private auction, and retreated into the darkest and dingiest quarters in the whole of Hertford College. There he became a dishevelled bohemian, took to lunching off hunks of bread and cheese and swallowing huge draughts of beer, and after dark often made Oxford ring with Falstaffian chants and objurgations.

In those days he was a vehement anti Papist; and he also conducted a noisy personal feud against various dons whom he particularly disliked. His moods were wild. On one occasion, having, in my absence, found his way into my rooms at Balliol, he finished a bottle of champagne that I had been unwise enough to leave behind me, and leaning from my fourth-floor window, above a quiet stretch of urban pavement, launched the empty bottle in the general direction of an inoffensive passer-by. I am sure that he meant to miss; luckily he did miss – though by a rather narrow margin. Seeing a bottle explode beneath his nose, the pedestrian hurried to the porter's lodge, where he delivered an impassioned protest. I was heavily fined by the college authorities. Had Evelyn's aim been a little more deliberate, his subsequent history, I suppose, might have taken a somewhat different turn.

As it was, once he had said goodbye to Oxford, he went

through a period of obscurity and tribulation. He was poor, in disgrace with his father, and though he was fond of drawing and carpentry, revealed no particular aptitude for any kind of profitable employment. He tried journalism; he was briefly a schoolmaster, but withdrew from the school after (he informed me) making facetious advances, on his way home from a convivial evening, to the stout and unattractive matron whom he encountered in a bedroom passage.

Then, just when his friends had begun to despair of him, he underwent a further change, fell in love, proposed, was married and set up as a contented householder, in a small, pretty house in an unfashionable district of London, furnished with an array of odd and charming knick-nacks. The habits of dandyism returned; I remember, at evening parties, his conspicuously stiff and gleaming shirt-front. His wife was as small and neat as himself. Side by side I thought that they resembled a pair of decorative pouter-pigeons. His first marriage, alas, was very soon to break down. The circumstances were humiliating; there is no doubt that he suffered deeply; and from this disaster he seems to have taken refuge in new beliefs and a new attitude towards the world that he continued to maintain until he died. I became aware myself of the transformation at a fairly early juncture.

Walking up St James's Street, I came face to face with him, accompanied by a rather grand young woman, his round pink features surmounted and almost eclipsed by an impressive top hat. I paused; his greeting was distant. In some confusion I admired his buttonhole – naturally, a small orchid; at which he pulled it out and suggested I might like to keep it – not, however as if he were making me a gift, but as if he had been distributing largesse to a needy old acquaintance. I forget if I refused or accepted. The great man nodded, smiled and passed on.

From that moment our friendship declined – partly, I must admit, because I had reviewed his biography of Dante Gabriel Rossetti less enthusiastically, or more critically, than he thought I should have done. But by that time the persona was firmly in place; and nothing – neither literary fame nor the success of his second marriage, which turned out to be as happy and prolific as his first marriage had been brief and barren – ever persuaded him to drop that strange disguise. Of all his books, one of the most revealing from a biographical point of view is 'The Ordeal of Gilbert Pinfold', his own lightly fictionalized account of how, in later life, he had once driven himself, by his reckless abuse of sleeping-pills and alcohol, right to the dizzy verge of nervous breakdown. Here he describes his persona at length, remarking, not without a touch of malicious glee, that many people found him 'formidable', and that his victims were apt to exchange anecdotes about his intimidating and aggressive manners.

Formidable he certainly was; and at this stage I can add a tale. Soon after he had returned from a journey to Hollywood, I was sitting beside a distinguished film-magnate, who, I presently ascertained, had undertaken to arrange his visit. What had he thought of the novelist, I inquired. Mr Waugh, he replied, in sorrowful tones, had gravely disappointed him. Why had he been disappointed? Well, it seemed that he had engaged for the celebrated visitor an especially splendid apartment in a particularly fine hotel. The apartment was to have been vacated a day before the novelist arrived. Then disaster struck. The previous occupants had been a delightful old married couple. The old man suddenly collapsed with a crippling paralytic stroke. The pair had been much loved; a wave of grief and consternation swept through the entire hotel. It had become clear that the invalid could not be moved, at least for another few hours, when Mr Waugh appeared at the hotel desk, looking very fierce and very authoritative, wearing his London bowler hat and grasping a tightly-rolled umbrella. The tragic situation was explained; profuse apologies, of course, were tendered. Mr Waugh refused to budge an inch; he continued loudly to demand his rooms. 'And do you know what he said?' I was asked. 'All Mr Waugh would say was "Your guests' health is no concern of mine!"'

Such was the Waugh persona at its most outrageous. So elaborate and so forbidding was its development in later years

that, if he were ill-disposed, his face came physically to suggest some kind of painted mask or visor – bulging eyes,
threatening sandy eyebrows, pendulous high-coloured
cheeks, pursed mouth and heavy florid jowl. But one must
bear in mind the element of self-parody. He loved to exagge-
rate his own disguises, and enjoyed playing the role of panto-
mime demon-king in which he had once decided he would
cast himself. As a journalist, he issued bizarre pronouncements, publicly regretting, for example, that the Spanish
Armada had failed to conquer England and thus – at no
matter what expense of life and liberty – restore his native
land to the authority of the Roman Catholic religion. He had
never, he announced, cast his vote in an election; the Queen
should be allowed to choose her own advisers. The modern
Welfare State was a pathetic farce; the care of the sick and
old and destitute was 'no concern' of any proper government.

Yet the novels showed us a different man. Although some
of his prejudices crept into his imaginative work, there he
usually had them under good control; and his professed con-
tempt for humanity had little effect on his method of drawing and analysing human character. Nor did the world-
weariness he so often advertised ever extinguish his prodigious sense of fun. True, the atmosphere of his latter books –
especially his admirable wartime series, *Men at Arms*, *Officers
and Gentlemen* and *Unconditional Surrender* – is dark with
despair and disillusionment; but he could always find room
for a comic intruder; and the vulgar and ridiculous Apthorpe
is almost as sympathetically depicted as an earlier hero, the
incomparable Captain Grimes.

In an obituary note, Graham Greene, with his usual generosity, has called Evelyn Waugh 'the greatest novelist of my
generation'. I believe he is right. No English novelist who
lived and worked during the first half of the twentieth
century has made a more distinctive contribution to the
literature of modern Europe. There are three standards, I assume, by which we can judge the lasting merits of a work of
fiction. Has the novelist introduced us to imaginary men and
women, who seem afterwards to have become a permanent

part of the world in which we live? Has his view of life changed or modified our own – so that, having read his book, we look at existence through slightly new eyes? Have his style and his method of narration had any real influence upon the ancient art of writing?

If these questions are applied to Evelyn Waugh, the answer in each case must be a bold affirmative. He was not an innovator; he distrusted innovations, and appears to have been perfectly content with the structure of the English novel as he found it. What he added were not fresh tricks of style – he was a soberly accomplished stylist – but a far subtler type of originality. Great imaginative talents generally arise from a conflict; and the hidden conflicts that made him so strange a man may also have helped to shape an extraordinarily gifted writer.

'The Colour of His Hair'

Two more remarkable and strangely divergent characters than the Kennedy Professor of Latin and the author of *A Shropshire Lad* and *Last Poems* have rarely inhabited the same body and sheltered behind a single name. The great Latinist was an almost perfect image of the scholarly recluse as popular legend represents him – dry, reserved, frequently sharp-tongued: the supreme authority on Manilius, an arid second-rate writer whose works his fellow Latinists very seldom troubled to explore, and whose chief literary merit is a knack of 'doing sums in verse': a lover of wine and good dinners, but often a moody, self-absorbed companion: above all, a secretive celibate fiercely attached to his personal privacy.

The author of *A Shropshire Lad*, on the other hand, gave the impression of being a wayward romantic, a man who had seen and suffered much, and had spent his early life in a round of vigorous rural pleasures, drinking and sometimes roistering with a group of handsome and hot-blooded comrades. Many of his closest friends had been exceptionally ill-starred; and their loss had caused him to develop a strain of vague autumnal melancholy, which made death by hanging and the suicide's fate particularly appealing subjects. When *Last Poems* appeared in 1922, twenty-six years after the publication of *A Shropshire Lad*, the poet's melancholy had acquired a deeper tone, and some of his pastoral pretences had been laid aside. But the 'golden lads', his beloved comrades of the past, still haunted his imagination, and thwarted desire and

169

irremediable loss were still the themes that stirred his creative energy.

Since each personage possessed conspicuous talents and their odd relationship has never been fully explained, it is not surprising that a literary analyst should at length have decided to enter the field and should have produced the kind of biographical study that A. E. Housman himself would probably have least welcomed.[1] The fault, however, was largely Housman's own. A writer who unfolds his sentimental history in a long series of poetic ideograms, where fact and fantasy seem to be combined with the deliberate intention of confusing the reader, must expect to arouse a good deal of curiosity about the personal background of his thoughts.

What were the origins of his mysterious sadness? Whence did he derive his obsession with the idea of death? Why did an air of impenetrable reserve gather around him during his later period? Houseman's biographer is clearly not in a position to answer all the reader's queries. But some he answers, and for some he suggests an answer, marshalling, and drawing deductions from, such scraps of evidence as are now available.

Housman, to begin with, was not a native of Shropshire; nor had he ever led a carefree rustic life. His actual birthplace was Bromsgrove, today absorbed into the suburbs of Birmingham, his father being a country solicitor, while his mother came of a clerical family settled in the Cotswolds. Edward Housman was a feckless parent who, battered by an unkind world, eventually took to heavy drinking; and Alfred Edward Housman appears to have despised his father but cherished and adored his mother, who succumbed to an agonizing disease when her son was twelve years old. Existence at Bromsgrove was drab and overclouded, though the distant outline of the Shropshire hills lay on the horizon like a land of promise; and the sensitive, talented, industrious boy longed to escape from this 'broken, disconsolate' household and breathe a fresher, more inspiring air. He went up to

[1]George L. Watson, *A. E. Housman: A Divided Life*, (Hart-Davis) 1957.

Oxford in 1877, but soon experienced a crushing and permanent reverse.

The protagonist of the drama that ensued was a stalwart youth named Moses John Jackson, an 'effortless honours student' and a 'natural athlete', one of those self-confident 'all-round men' who treat the whole world as their willing football. Jackson appreciated Housman's qualities; but Housman evidently worshipped Jackson; and his adoration (according to the poet's new biographer) threatened to defy control and to pass beyond the proper limits. Jackson, of course, found it impossible to respond – at least as fervently as his friend wished. His method of handling a difficult situation was characterized (Housman's biographer assumes) by a mixture of instinctive humanity and delicate intuitive tact.

He 'jollied his friend along', to use an idiom that he might himself have employed, hoping that the errant admirer would eventually regain his senses. But Housman never recovered his senses, so far as the idol he had chosen, his 'kind and foolish comrade', was concerned, even though, after they had both left Oxford, Jackson announced his engagement to an eminently suitable young woman who bore him happy, healthy children, severed his link with England and accepted a teaching post in Northern India. Housman agreed to dismissal but could not stifle his sorrow or forget his defeat. He commemorated them in some revelatory lines printed among his *Last Poems*:

> Because I liked you better
> Than suits a man to say,
> It irked you, and I promised
> To throw the thought away.
>
> To put the world between us
> We parted stiff and dry;
> 'Good-bye,' said you, 'forget me.'
> 'I will, no fear,' said I.

The crisis that followed Housman's recognition of his inveterate emotional tendencies may have been responsible for his astonishing failure to pass his Oxford Finals and the temporary breakdown of his academic career. The brilliant undergraduate, ignominiously ploughed, was condemned to more than a decade of Civil Service drudgery. During those years, however, he seems to have determined on a line of moral conduct. Among the documents he preserved to the end of his life was a report, cut from a daily newspaper, of the pathetic message that an eighteen-year-old Woolwich cadet had composed just before his suicide. His motives (the young man told the Coroner) included a sense of 'utter cowardice and despair. There is only one thing ... which could make me thoroughly happy; that one thing I have no earthly hope of obtaining. ... I have absolutely ruined my own life; but I thank God that ... I have not morally injured ... anyone else. Now I am quite certain that I could not live another five years without doing so. ...'

Housman's brother Laurence discovered this cutting pressed between the pages of a poem, the forty-fourth poem in *A Shropshire Lad*:

> Shot? so quick, so clean an ending?
> Oh that was right, lad, that was brave:
> Yours was not an ill for mending,
> 'Twas best to take it to the grave.

The ill that he could not mend, and could only partially sublimate with the help of literature, he determined that he must bury at a depth from which it would never re-emerge. One of his posthumously published poems is yet more significant – the fable of the young man with oddly coloured hair, written in 1895, the year of Oscar Wilde's tragedy:

Oh who is that young sinner with the handcuffs on his wrists?
And what has he been after that they groan and shake their fists?
And wherefore is he wearing such a conscience-stricken air?
Oh they're taking him to prison for the colour of his hair.

Having once recognized the 'colour of his hair', Housman gradually resigned himself to a life of scholarship and solitude. That, in brief, is his biographer's thesis; and, although a good many passages of his book are based upon inspired guesswork he has produced a notably vivid and deeply sympathetic picture. We need not, I think, regret his temerity: Housman's reputation is sufficiently well founded to warrant intensive personal research. True, he was a minor poet; but he had a highly individual talent. He can be parodied: he cannot be imitated. The literary style he evolved could be handled by no other writer, with its odd blend of classical and modern elements, its lilting – almost jaunty – music, its touches of superficial pessimism and the heartfelt melancholy of the underlying refrain. Mr Watson's description of the man who created that style deserves to be read by all who have enjoyed his work.

Robert Graves

The future historian who takes as his subject the first half of the twentieth century may find, when he comes to investigate the psychological background of the period, that much turns on the dramatic difference between the character of the two World Wars. During the nightmare summer days of 1939, as we watched the sandbags filled, saw the barrage balloons rise and heard the earliest sirens wail, we most of us expected an even grimmer repetition of the conflict that had begun in 1914. Horrible enough the actual conflict was. But it did not, with the same mechanical thoroughness, destroy a great, and perhaps the best, part of an entire generation; and upon the majority of those who survived the effect that it produced seems to have been far slighter and more transitory. I have known otherwise sensitive men who would admit that they 'quite enjoyed' the last war, which whirled them to and fro across seas and continents, and allowed them lengthy spells of leisure and pleasure in the intervals of fear and danger. No moderately civilized person could have pretended to enjoy the previous struggle; the mental scars that it left behind it could often be distinguished throughout a whole lifetime.

Among the damaged survivors of World War I were a number of the so-called 'Georgian Poets'. They had become war poets in the trenches of Northern France; and war poets – writers, that is to say, shaped and still profoundly moved by their experiences – they remained for the next ten or fifteen years. Thus Robert Graves has described his meetings with Siegfried Sassoon and Edmund Blunden, at a time when the war had run its course, but all three of them were still living under a heavy cloud of war neurosis. Graves had also described the tragic intensity of his own feelings – and how, walking down a London street, he would see the pavement littered with the bodies of the fallen: how 'shells used to come bursting on my bed at midnight', and 'strangers in day-time would assume the faces of friends who had been killed'.

Complete scenes, taken out of the past, were perpetually sliding back into the present day: 'The war was not over for us yet.... I would have a sudden very clear experience of men on the march up the Béthune-La Bassée road....' Or he would imagine that he was still in a dug-out at Cambrin: 'I would look up the shaft and see somebody's muddy legs coming down the steps, and there would be a crash and the tobacco-smoke in the dug-out would shake with the concussion and twist about in patterns like the marbling on books.' Day-dreams of the kind did not cease to trouble him 'until well on in 1928'.

Hundreds of thousands of young men must have shared the same agonies. But to a similar crisis every human being is bound to respond in a slightly different fashion; and Robert Graves was even then an artist, with an artist's heightened nervous susceptibility. He was the product, moreover, of a gifted and unusual line, which included a Cromwellian regicide and that remarkably eccentric eighteenth-century parson, the author of *The Spiritual Quixote*, who held and propagated some peculiar views on marriage and the education of children. And then, although we might be justified in regarding him as a typically 'English' writer, Graves' descent was not completely English.

His father, a hard-worked Inspector of Schools, but in his spare moments a frequenter of late-Victorian literary society, combined Scottish and Irish Protestant strains; while his mother was of German stock, the niece of the celebrated historian Leopold von Ranke, who declared that he was an historian before he was a Christian, and that his object in writing historical works was 'simply to find out how things actually occurred'. An inherited passion for discovering how events

176

actually took place seems to have prompted the composition of his grand-nephew's well-known historical novels – except that von Ranke was an historical scientist, and Robert Graves, being first and foremost an imaginative artist, has never had much use for the strictly scientific method.

Judging from his autobiography, *Goodbye to All That* – an uncommonly revealing, if somewhat patchy and uneven book – the poet's childhood was, on the whole, pleasant; and he owed much not only to his literary father but to his original and entertaining mother, whom I dimly recollect as a vague, but determined, old lady, with a large generous soul and her noble Teutonic head among the clouds. As for his schooldays at Charterhouse, they appear to have followed the customary English pattern; and he might perhaps, when he left school, have slipped into some quiet official or academic job, had World War I not exploded and swept him headlong into the British army, where he soon established his position as a brave and competent young officer. Thus an important stage was arbitrarily removed from his existence: without the usual period of transition and preparation, the promising schoolboy was obliged to face terrible adult responsibilities; and, when peace was declared, he had still, in some respects, an almost adolescent point of view. Idealistic, sternly puritanical, he had acquired a fund of curious knowledge and experience that had little bearing on the facts of ordinary civilian life.

Graves' puritanism has certainly died hard, despite the varying fortunes of his personal career. His first love, he tells us, ended in bitter disillusionment; 'Dick', the handsome boy he had loved at school – but loved with romantic and platonic fervour – was unmasked as a practising homosexual while his admirer was on active service. 'Dick,' he heard, 'was not at all the innocent sort of fellow I took him for. He was as bad as anyone could be.' Later, he learned that 'Dick' had appeared at a police court, accused of attempting to seduce a soldier. 'This news was nearly the end of me'; but he did his best to rationalize the situation by deciding that the war had driven his idol mad. The poet's horror of homosexuality is expressed in various post-war writings. It may perhaps have stimulated his cult of the Female Principle under the fearsome symbol of the White Goddess.

When I visited him at his cottage near Oxford about 1923 or 1924, he had not yet emerged from his puritanical phase – he announced that an immoral man could never be a good poet; nor had he yet been able to cast off the neurotic legacy of his war adventures. But he was already engaged, slowly and patiently, in accomplishing his own salvation; and he had evolved an odd and original theory about the nature and purpose of a poet's work. Every poem was the solution of a problem that could not otherwise be formulated and re-solved. 'I regarded poetry (he informs us in *Goodbye to All That*) as, first, a personal cathartic for the poet suffering from some inner conflict, and then as a cathartic for readers in a similar conflict. I made a tentative connection between poetry and dream in the light of the dream psychology in which I was then interested as a means of curing myself.'

His earlier verses – for example, the 'collection of ro-mantic poems and ballads' entitled *Country Sentiment* – were often primarily poems of escape, through which the poet took refuge from the painful present in realms of decorative literary make-believe; and they were sometimes marred, he felt at a later stage, by 'falsities for public delectation'. *The Pier Glass*, on the other hand, represented a courageous effort to follow the ghosts that haunted him down the corridors of his own mind, and trace them to their secret, far-off lairs. Yet – a significant point – he did not wish completely to exor-cise all these ghostly influences: 'Somehow I thought that the power of writing poetry, which was more important to me than anything else I did, would disappear if I allowed myself to get cured; my *Pier Glass* haunting would end and I would become merely a dull easy writer.' In fact, long after he had outlived the period of war neurosis, he continued to keep ghostly company; and it is remarkable how many references to ghosts and phantasmal lore are to be found in his latest volume of collected verse. As a mature writer, he holds a successful balance between the luminous and the obscure, the rational and the irrational aspects of his poetic personality.

Meanwhile he had married and begotten children, his wife being the very young daughter of that highly expert painter William Nicholson, and of Mabel Nicholson, also a talented artist, sister to James Pryde, with whom Nicholson had formerly collaborated in the production of commercial posters and a gallery of modern wood-cut portraits. One of Max Beerbohm's closest friends, Nicholson was a dandy of the same stamp. Small, self-assured, whimsical, alert, he affected high starched collars and long beautifully laundered cuffs, pearl-buttoned waistcoats yellow or speckled, jauntily slanted hats and dazzling patent-leather shoes. It was typical of Nicholson's sense of fun that, when his daughter and son-in-law ran into serious financial difficulties, he should have folded a hundred pound note inside an ordinary match-box and sent it to them through the post.

Despite his dandyism, he was an extremely masculine character; and, like other daughters of particularly virile men, Nancy Nicholson – who, after marriage, had insisted on retaining her maiden name – turned out to be an ardent feminist. She believed that the work of the household should be divided equally between wife and husband; and Graves' early books were planned and composed with his children – there were soon four of them – playing or scrambling around his feet, in an atmosphere of boiling saucepans, drying towels and water heating for the baby's bath. Money was always short: the poet and his entire family lived on about two hundred pounds a year. Yet Graves bore little resemblance to Hogarth's picture of 'The Distressed Poet'. Family life seemed to suit his temperament, and certainly never impaired his temper – he has a naturally domestic, even a mildly patriarchal turn; while his wife's feminism, far from irking him, was at length absorbed into his own philosophy.

This period of the writer's existence – during which he lived, first at a cottage that belonged to John Masefield, on Boars Hill, overlooking Oxford, where he and his wife made a sadly unprofitable attempt to conduct the local shop; afterwards, at the nearby village of Islip – came to an abrupt end in 1926. He was then offered, and decided to accept, a newly founded Chair of English Literature at an Egyptian government university. The salary attached was fourteen hundred pounds per annum – a huge sum by the poet's modest standards, so huge that it emboldened him to suggest that a young American poetess of the day, Laura Riding Gottschalk, with whom he had established contact, I think, through another American poet, John Crowe Ransom, should leave home, cross the Atlantic and join the Graves family on their Near-Eastern pilgrimage.

Thus began a momentous literary partnership that lasted until 1939, of which the opening stages are allusively celebrated in the postscript to his autobiographical volume, while its conclusion is briefly mentioned in his preface to *The Common Asphodel*. Laura Riding, as she soon re-named herself, was – and, no doubt, still is – a decidedly formidable personage, whose influence over the friends and disciples whom she gathered round her can only be compared to that of Madame de Staël over the little group at Coppet. Physically, too, there may have been some likeness. Both were shock-headed, square-built women, with large powerfully compulsive eyes; both excited alarm as well as respect, and were treated by their admiring associates with all the deference due to a contemporary sibyl. In 1927, the autobiographer notes, 'Nancy and I suddenly parted company'. By that time, he had also parted with most of the 'leading and subsidiary characters' depicted in *Goodbye to All That*; and, having cleared the stage, he embarked on a new relationship that dominated his life and work for many years to come. Its setting was the island of Majorca until the outbreak of the Spanish Civil War, subsequently a small château in the North of France and a farm near New Hope in the United States.

Simultaneously, his verse grew more sparse and austere, his critical prose writings more prophetic and dogmatic in tone. Every genuine poet seems to incorporate several contrasted but complementary selves; and, beside the carefree Imaginative Artist, Robert Graves includes the Pedant and the Prophet, the last presumably being a relic of his Celtic inheritance, while the Pedant obviously derives from his learned German forbears. Like D. H. Lawrence, in his search for a new society he was constantly groping towards a new religion; and, at this stage, when he had bidden farewell to the past, his utterances were sometimes profoundly obscure, even unexpectedly pretentious – witness the strange paragraphs with which he brings to an end the moving story of his early life. Ordinary events acquired a transcendental meaning. I remember, for example, how one day I happened to meet William Nicholson in the street outside his studio. He looked gloomy. 'We've just had a postcard from Robert and Laura, to say that they are leaving for Spain together to *stop Time*', he reported with a dubious shake of the head.

Yet, if the influence of Laura Riding accentuated his prophetic tendency – and if the prophet's pronouncements were apt to be rather dark and tangled – it also impelled him to sharpen the edge of his style, to think more deeply and carefully about the exact value of the words he used in verse; and it was counterbalanced by his instinctive affection for vivid, concrete, sensuous images. Laura Riding's intellectualism – often somewhat arid in her own poems – helped to remove from his verse the last touches of Georgian sentimentalism. Neither poetry nor prophesy could settle his economic problem; and from 1934 onwards he published the famous series of historical novels that began with *I, Claudius* and *Claudius the God*. But the poet was always incensed should the novelist receive undue attention. He dismissed his best-selling novels as pot-boilers, written chiefly with the object of producing a quick financial dividend.

That they are much more than pot-boilers, every critic will agree; though again and again he may find himself disputing Robert Graves' interpretations of the past. Personally, I have always thought of the Roman Empire as an immense, complex, often cruel but, on the whole, smoothly running piece of bureaucratic mechanism, which continued to operate efficiently even at times when a sadistic madam happened to occupy the Palatine Hill; during the reign of Nero, for example, the Roman provinces are said to have been particularly well-administered. Graves prefers to emphasize the human element, with all its individual waywardness. His Romans have a faintly rustic air – beneath the toga emerge a pair of hobnailed boots; and, in his text, the meetings of the Senate are apt to suggest the confabulations of an Oxfordshire Rural District Council. His generals are English infantry officers; and the Emperor he chose as the hero of his first two books was one of the homeliest and crankiest members of his tragic and eccentric family.

Not content with re-creating the past through the medium of imaginative fiction, Graves has also developed a taste for revising, refurnishing and re-writing the literary records that it left behind. He is among the foremost re-writers of the age – here the Pedant and the Prophet combine their efforts. In 1933, he published *The Real David Copperfield*, illustrating how Dickens might, and ought to, have designed his masterpiece, had he been unimpeded by Victorian social conventions; in 1953 – a yet more ambitious effort – he 'restored' *The Nazarene Gospel*, a revised version of the New Testament, stripped of tendentious Pauline glosses; and in 1955 came the turn of *The Greek Myths*, to which he endeavoured to give back their ancient simplicity and dignity of meaning, with the help of the abstruse wisdom he had imbibed at the footstool of the White Goddess.

The focal point of all his scholarly researches is the bizarre theory of Analeptic Thought, based on his belief that forgotten events may be recovered by the exercise of intuition, which affords sudden glimpses of truth 'that could not have been arrived at by inductive reasoning'. In practice, of course, this sometimes means that the historian first decides what he would *like* to believe, then looks around for facts to suit his thesis. According to a classical scholar I once consulted, although his facts themselves are usually sound, they do not always support the elaborate conclusions that Graves proceeds to draw from them; two plus two regularly make five and six; and genuine erudition and prophetic imagination conspire to produce some very odd results.

Robert Graves

Certainly *The White Goddess* is an extraordinarily baffling volume – a bold attempt to dethrone Apollo and Zeus, and the poetic standards they exemplify, in favour of a much more venerable godhead, the Mediterranean Mother Goddess, prototype of the Muse whom every 'Chief Poet' serves with a mixture of exaltation and alarm. The young poet who ceases to write verse may have forfeited his literary birthright because he has lost his sense of that formidable divinity : 'The woman whom he took to be a Muse, or who was a Muse, turns into a domestic woman and would have him turn similarly into a domesticated man. . . .' For the White Goddess, he explains, 'is anti-domestic; she is the perpetual "other woman", and her part is difficult indeed for a woman of sensibility to play for more than a few years', because the desire to abandon her true rôle and 'commit suicide in simple domesticity lurks in every muse's and maenad's heart'.

Whatever its limitations may be as a work of historical research or literary scholarship – one is surprised to learn that only two English writers, John Skelton and Ben Jonson, deserve to be considered 'Chief Poets'; and there is an unfortunate slip at the beginning of Chapter 25 about the Aztecs and the Incas – *The White Goddess* will prove an admirable source-book for all who wish to study the writer's personal development and hope to understand his poetry. In his opening sentence, he makes a proud claim: 'Since the age of fifteen poetry has been my ruling passion and I have never intentionally undertaken any task or formed any relationship that seemed inconsistent with poetic principles. . . .' Prose-writing has provided a means of livelihood; but he has employed it 'as a means of sharpening my sense of the altogether different nature of poetry, and the themes that I choose are always linked in my mind with outstanding poetic problems'.

That claim, I think, is perfectly justified, at least in so far as it concerns his single-minded, lifelong devotion to the art of poetry; for, if Robert Graves now stands high above the great majority of modern English poets, he owes his position not only to his inherited gifts but to the remarkable persistence and diligence with which he has exploited them. He has turned out an enormous quantity of prose – much of it extremely good prose; yet it is difficult to imagine him as anything but a professional poet, whose sheer professionalism is no less conspicuous than the imaginative zeal with which he serves his art. We may discount a good deal of his pedantic and prophetic theorizing; his volume of collected verse remains, and his poems speak their own language.

Today Robert Graves has passed his seventieth birthday – he was born in 1895 – a tall, robust, grizzle-headed figure, with a broken nose, like Michelangelo's, and a greyish-pallid untanned Northern skin. He still lives on the rocky shores of Majorca, in the stone-walled, tile-roofed house that he designed and built himself about a thousand feet above the sea. Behind it the mountains rise up steep and grim; and around the house is a grove of fragrant orange-trees and lemon-trees. Though much more spacious than once at Islip, his way of life is unextravagant. At least, he works unconscionably hard; and, although a saucepan on the hob no longer divides his attention with his books and manuscripts, he still writes in furious bursts of energy, often leaving his desk to pace the floor or wander through the house and garden.

His talk is vigorous and idiosyncratic, usually prefaced by a bold assertion, concerning the 'real truth', as he sees it, about some question of topical or historical interest; for, like Sir Thomas Browne, he is much preoccupied with putting right the 'vulgar errors' of our age. Incidentally, he is a believer in signs and portents. He has never lost his sense of mystery, his instinctive feeling for the numinous; and he uses the Islamic word *baraka*, as he once explained in a paper read at a meeting of the American Academy and National Institute of Letters, to denote the natural magic that may distinguish 'almost anything', from a battered old metal cooking pot to a modern poem or the King James' Bible.

Just as the Bible, in the latest English version, has been purged of its antique numinous quality, so he finds that the twentieth-century world is gradually losing its primitive sense of wonder. In his own poetry that sense of wonder persists – wonder combined with delight and dread. Like every true imaginative artist, he shows us trees as men, and men as trees walking, and helps to break down the rigid conceptual pattern, imposed on the ordinary unpoetic mind by years of lethargy and acquiescent habit. Again like every good poet, he has both an individual view of existence and a correspondingly individual style. 'Genuine modernists (he has written) do not make individual style their object: they try to write each poem in the way which fits it best. But the sum of their work has individuality because of their natural variousness. . . . True style is the personal handwriting in which poetry is written; if it can be easily imitated or reduced to a formula it should be at once suspect to the poets themselves.'

Robert Graves, as a writer of verse, is both uncommonly various and unusually flexible. Perhaps the variety is most apparent; in the paperback edition of his collected verse that I have recently been looking through, I see that I have marked at random poems on Ulysses, a butterfly, the art of storytelling, war-memories, the priapic principle, lover's speech, deception in love, cat-goddesses, bears, the Majorcan sirocco and the communiqué that Persian press-officers probably issued about the Persian failure to conquer Greece – the last inspired, I am told, by a British failure to land on the coast of German-occupied France.

Here the 'natural variousness' of the poet's mind produces without question an effect of stylistic individuality. Yet, although each poem is a separate unit, existing in its own right, together these units form a continuous record of the poet's mental odyssey, from Ithaca, the scene of his childhood, through the hideous storms of war, past many Circean islets and round again across still troubled waters. Odysseus did not expect that he would reach his final goal; nor presumably does Robert Graves. Meanwhile he continues to keep a log, written up (he tells us) 'at the fairly constant rate' of four or five poems a year since 1914. The record is lyrical, yet never devoid of wit – he employs wit as successfully as the seventeenth-century Metaphysical poet; and he, too, is personal and satiric without sacrificing his persuasive lyric flow.

If we are to enjoy him as he deserves to be enjoyed – and the merits of a poem can only be gauged by the quality and the duration of the pleasure it gives – his poems should be read in bulk. A survivor of the *Georgian Book* period, he alone among his immediate contemporaries – and, indeed, among representatives of the post-war literary age – has contrived to hold a steady onward course. At no juncture is its line broken, as the lines of the human hand are broken; his poetic 'Line of Destiny' is astonishingly straight and clear. The ghosts have receded, though they have not completely vanished; love, always an obsessive preoccupation, continues to excite his analytical instincts, as it once excited those of Donne; and this 'near-honourable malady' is the subject of many of his latest poems. How much does he owe to World War I? By overcoming that traumatic experience, he gained the strength and the sense of direction he needed; and he himself seemed to acknowledge the debt he owed when he visited London in 1961. Questioned by a pertinacious journalist, he sent up the customary controversial kite. What was wrong with England today? The younger generation, he suggested was subconsciously looking forward to, and feeling the lack of, yet another international conflict. This theory, under a slightly different form, he repeated in 1969.

John Falstaff: A Biography

Sir John Falstaff – 'Jack Falstaff with my familiars, John with my brothers and sisters, and Sir John with all Europe' – died, a broken old man, during the early months of 1415. We know regrettably little of his early life – almost as little as we know of the childhood and boyhood of his great exponent William Shakespeare. Even the date of his birth remains mysterious. But he entered the world, he once informed a company, 'about three of the clock in the afternoon'; and, as, in 1402, he announced that his years were 'some fifty, or by 'r lady, inclining to three score,' it cannot have been much later than 1346, when King Edward III's invincible English bowmen picked off the French knights upon the field of Crécy.

Perhaps a Falstaff sat at the King's side and watched the advancing cavalry tumbled from their chargers. Shakespeare's hero came of ancient feudal stock; he began his education by serving as page in the household of Thomas Mowbray, Duke of Norfolk. So reported his admirer Justice Shallow; but then, Shallow's memory may have been growing vague. Norfolk at the time was still a beardless boy; and the magnate whom Falstaff served was probably the Duke's father, John de Mowbray, Earl of Nottingham.

Next, we catch sight of him at the London Inns of Court; and there, we learn, he cut a dashing figure. The law students were a wild disorderly crew; and he and Shallow, both of Clement's Inn, with their chosen companions – 'little John Doit of Staffordshire, and black George Barnes, and Francis Pickbone, and Will Squele, a Cotswold man' – rivalled the most celebrated 'swinge-bucklers' of their age. 'Hem boys!'

was their watchword, as they drank and fought and womanized. Shallow remembered seeing Falstaff 'break Skogan's head at the court-gate when a' was a crack not thus high,' the same day that he himself did battle with 'one Sampson Stockfish, a fruiterer, behind Gray's Inn'. Every attractive and accessible girl of the neighbourhood was entered on the friend's books. 'I may say to you,' Shallow told his cousin, long after he had retired to Gloucestershire and become a sober justice of the peace, 'we knew where the bona robas were, and had the best of them all at commandment.'

Those were mad days, followed by adventurous nights. During that century – indeed, for centuries later – meadows and orchards closely surrounded London. Citizens passed through its battlemented gates straight into the open country, where cattle grazed and milkmaids filled their pails, archers practised at the butts, and weavers and fullers hung out their cloths to dry. Amid the rural districts north of the City's precincts, law students and London apprentices often played or raised riots; and once, as Shallow recollected, he and Falstaff had lain 'all night in the windmill in Saint George's field'. Presumably they had got drunk and, when they began to wander home, found the gates already closed. At least, they had slept in the mill, upon the miller's dusty bales, and listened to the deep-toned bells of the City ringing out from a hundred different steeples. Falstaff agreed that he had not forgotten the episode: 'We have heard the chimes at midnight, Master Shallow.' Nor had he lost sight of Jane Nightwork, a famous bona roba they had known. 'She could never away with me,' Shallow admitted. 'Never, never; she would always say she could not abide Master Shallow.' 'By the mass, I could anger her to the heart. . . . Doth she hold her own well?' At which Falstaff ruefully shook his head: 'Old, old, Master Shallow.'

So much for an enjoyably ill-spent youth; but Falstaff's middle years are wrapped in deep obscurity. He reappears as an ageing man, dissolute crony of the scape-grace Prince and centre of a Bohemian gang that had established its London headquarters at the Boar's-Head, Eastcheap. Falstaff had been a slender, graceful stripling. '. . . When I was about thy years, Hal,' he assured the Prince, 'I was not an eagle's talon in the waist; I could have crept into an alderman's thumb-ring. . . .' Indeed, though considerably better-looking, he was nearly as slight as the skeletonious Shallow; of whom Falstaff would later remark that, at Clement's Inn, he had been 'like a man made after supper of a cheese paring: when a' was naked, he was, for all the world, like a forked radish, with a head fantastically carved upon it with a knife: a' was so forlorn, that his dimensions to any thick sight were invisible: a' was the very genius of famine; yet lecherous as a monkey, and the whores called him mandrake. . . .'

During middle life, however, Falstaff had become immensely large; and he himself chose to attribute his transformation to the psychosomatic effects of sorrow and anxiety – to long experience of 'sighing and grief'; which, he declared blew a man up bladderwise. In fact, he claimed to be suffering from what our modern psychiatrists call bulimia, or a compulsive tendency to eat. But this explanation seems a trifle far-fetched. John Falstaff, in every other respect, was a thoroughly well-balanced person: no thin man was clamouring to get out from that gigantic and misshapen body; and a biographer may prefer to believe that, if his paunch expanded – 'How long is't ago, Jack,' demanded his royal patron, 'since thou sawest thine own knee?' – it was because he always avoided exercise, had a hearty appetite for roast capon and a prodigious thirst for sweet wines.

An Eastcheap tavern bill that has come down to us indicates the bulk and richness of his meals:

Item, A capon	...	...	...	2s.	2d.
Item, Sauce ...	...	...	...		4d.
Item, Sack, two gallons	...	...	5s.	8d.
Item, Anchovies and sack after supper		2s.	6d.
Item, bread ...	...	...	...		ob.

'O monstrous!' commented the Prince, 'but one half-penny-worth of bread to this intolerable deal of sack.' Falstaff, we learn, was also a heavy sleeper, who would spend his afternoons stretched out on a bench, or take refuge behind the arras on the tavern walls, where he was discovered 'snorting like a horse'.

Yet, with all this, he had kept his power to charm. Otherwise, besides dominating his social inferiors, how could he have fasincated a selfish and capricious young man who expected to ascend the throne of England? He cannot have succeeded by social buffoonery alone. Shakespeare's portrait sufficiently underlines Falstaff's native strength of character – not only his constant gaiety and perpetually resourceful wit, but his warmth, worldly wisdom, human kindliness and his gift of inspiring and retaining love. Did the Prince love him? Well, at least as much as that somewhat callous youth could experience any disinterested emotion. Certainly, Falstaff loved the Prince, with the same romantic half-paternal feeling that bound Menenius Agrippa to Coriolanus, and may possibly have attached Shakespeare to the extravagant young grandee, Lord Southampton. In Prince Henry, Falstaff found a son; while Falstaff became a travestied father-figure who established a dominant hold upon the young man's mind.

Their relationship is difficult to analyse – until we recollect that Prince Henry's bodily father was a frigid, gloomy, guilt-obsessed sovereign, who could never forget that he had displaced the rightful king and had seized the crown by craft and violence. With Falstaff, his substitute father, Prince Henry was on a much more comfortable footing. Here was a fatherly image he need neither fear nor respect, the focus at once of his thwarted affection and of the secret filial antagonism he could not elsewhere show. Thus the Prince often mocked Falstaff, as at times he may have wished to mock his parent; and it amused him to parody their relation by promoting Falstaff to the King's rôle, and by kneeling at his feet on the boards of the Eastcheap tavern, while Falstaff delivered a solemn parental lecture:

'Harry, I do not only marvel where thou spendest thy time, but also how thou art accompanied. ... That thou art my son, I have partly they mother's word, partly my own opinion, but chiefly a villainous trick of thine eye, and a foolish hanging

of thy nether lip. ... If then thou be son to me ... why ... art
thou so pointed at? ... Pitch, as ancient writers do report, doth
defile: so doth the company thou keepest. ... And yet there is
a virtuous man whom I have often noted in thy company, but
I know not his name.'

'What manner of man, an it like your majesty?'

'A goodly portly man, i'faith, and a corpulent; of a cheerful
look, a pleasing eye, and a most noble carriage ... and now
I remember me, his name in Falstaff: if that man should be
lewdly given, he deceiveth me; for, Harry, I see virtue in his
looks.'

Round the actors in this remarkable scene were gathered
the raffish frequenters of the Boar's-Head – sharp Poins, the
Prince's favoured crony; carbuncular Bardolph; Gadshill, a
professional cutpurse; Peto, a nondescript hanger-on; and
Mistress Nell Quickly, the middle-aged owner of the house.
Just how Falstaff had sunk to these depths his chronicler does
not explain. He still occasionally appeared in courtly, even
royal, circles; but no doubt he preferred the company of inferiors, who admired and respected him, to that of his equals
and superiors who, now that he was ageing and short of
credit, frequently looked down on him. Moreover, it is clear
from his record that he had a natural taste for low life.

This taste he shared with the Prince himself; and Falstaff
was delighted to act as the young man's guide through some
of the entertaining byways of the London underworld. Com-
mitting 'the oldest sins the newest kind of ways' was Prince
Henry's chief pastime. The sins he practised included high-
way robbery; and, during the summer of the year 1402, the
Prince, Poins, Falstaff, Bardolph and Gadshill (who gave the
operation a professional touch) all engaged in a celebrated
attempt to hold up travellers on the pilgrim road to Canter-
bury, where the Prince and Poins arranged to attack their
accomplices and drove them headlong from the field of
action. After a blow or two, Falstaff gave ground and, as he
struggled to gain a place of safety, 'larded the lean earth with
sweat. ...'

Then, while he was telling his story of the crowd of opponents he had fought and worsted – 'I am eight times thrust through the doublet, four through the hose ... my sword hacked like a hand-saw – *ecce signum*! I never dealt the better since I was a man' – news reached London that the powerful Percy clan, headed by Hotspur, 'that same mad fellow of the north,' had joined the Welsh rebel Owen Glendower and had taken up arms against the King's government. This period of national emergency lasted until the following summer; and Falstaff, thanks to the Prince's patronage, was entrusted with 'a charge of foot' – which shows that his military reputation was not yet smirched beyond repair; and he thereupon went off to the Midlands, where he set about recruiting infantry.

The operation proved extremely successful; in Falstaff's hands it became a lucrative racket, which earned him 'three hundred and odd pounds'. For his method was to enlist 'none but good householders, yeomen's sons ... toasts-and-butter, with hearts in their bellies no bigger than pins' heads,' allow them to buy themselves out of service and fill their places by pressing half-starved yokels. Thus he presently collected 'a hundred and fifty tattered prodigals', at whose head even their commander felt ashamed to march through Coventry. Nevertheless he led them into battle, saw his ragamuffins soundly peppered and not three of the contingent left alive. After which, in a sudden burst of courage, he ventured to cross swords with Douglas but, finding he was greatly outmatched, sensibly decided that he would play possum. As he lay there, his carcass was espied by the Prince, whose valediction seems unexpectedly generous from so self-centred and unimaginative a character:

> 'What, old acquaintance! could not all this flesh
> Keep in a little life? Poor Jack, farewell!
> I could have better spared a better man....'

But Falstaff went too far by pretending that he had accounted for Hotspur and lugging in the fallen warrior's corpse.

The Battle of Shrewsbury was fought on July 21, 1403; and the second half of Shakespeare's dramatic chronicle covers the years between that date and April 1413. In Falstaff's career, despite his habitual sloth, it was a decade of almost continuous activity. Having returned to London from the wars, he had an alarming encounter with the Lord Chief Justice, but boldly countered the magistrate's reprimand by asserting that gay intemperance was natural to the spring of life: 'You that are old consider not the capacities of us who are young. . . .' He was also arrested for debt at the suit of Mistress Quickly, while he was on his way to dine with Master Smooth the silkman, beneath – Mistress Quickly's version of the address – the sign of 'the Lubber's-Head in Lumbert Street', a predicament from which he escaped only by a grand display of gentlemanly bluff and a shrewd appeal to his creditor's tenderest feelings. And, that same summer, when a second revolt broke out, headed by Northumberland and other factious English lords, Falstaff again headed for the country and, with Bardolph as his capable lieutenant, practised his old game of recruiting likely yokels.

There he encountered his boyhood's friend Shallow, Gloucestershire magnate and sententious justice of the peace; and the two elderly gentlemen indulged in delightful recollections of the wild days they had spent at Clement's Inn. From Gloucestershire he marched his troop to Yorkshire, joined the royal forces at Gaultree Forest, saw service in the ensuing battle, personally received the surrender of a knight named Colville of the Dale, 'a most furious knight and valorous enemy', who, no doubt, paid a large ransom, but was heavily snubbed by Prince Henry's younger brother, the priggish martinet, Prince John of Lancaster.

It took more than a princely reproof to damp Falstaff's naturally ebullient spirits. He had now re-established his renown as a 'man of action' and a 'man of war'; and he reappears early in 1413 on another visit to his friend Shallow. This was the zenith of Falstaff's progress; Henry IV was fast approaching his end, and the Prince's favourite cheerfully looked ahead to a new life of unlimited power and prosperity. Shallow, too, lived in high hopes – 'a friend i' the court is better than a penny in purse'; and the dinner he ordered at his rustic manor house was proportionally extravagant: 'Some pigeons, Davy, a couple of short-legged hens, a joint of mutton, and any pretty little tiny kickshaws, tell William cook.'

After dinner, the company retired to the orchard, to 'eat a last year's pippin, with a dish of caraways', where Shallow's tongue-tied cousin Silence burst into raucous tipsy song and, at Falstaff's direction, was carried off to bed. Before he had been removed, there was a violent knocking on the door; and then, in stalked Falstaff's ensign Pistol – one of those loud-voiced, long-sworded, down-at-heel soldiers who then hung about St Paul's Church – to inform his commander that the moribund King was dead. 'Sweet knight,' Pistol proclaimed triumphantly, 'thou art now one of the great men in this realm.'

Falstaff's response was prompt and characteristic; without unnecessary delay he borrowed a thousand pounds from Justice Shallow, offering him any official position that he chose, marshalled the company, called for his horse and went thundering back along the road to London. As soon as he reached Westminster, he hastened to the Abbey precincts, where heralds were clearing the road and servants of the Court were strewing rushes, and, wedged into the dense crowd with Shallow, Pistol and Bardolph, waited on tenter-hooks to cheer the new sovereign. At length Henry v emerged among his attendants, but a statelier, grimmer, very different Henry, a remote, processional, richly cloaked personage, blind at first to the old man's bows and smiles, deaf to his impassioned salutations. Thrice Falstaff was obliged to repeat his cry: 'God save thy Grace, King Hal! My royal Hal . . . God save thee, my sweet boy! . . . my King! my Jove! I speak to thee, my heart!' – before the crushing, callous blow descended:

'I know thee not, old man: fall to thy prayers. . . .
Reply not to me with a fool-born jest:
Presume not that I am the thing I was;
For God doth know, so shall the world perceive,
That I have turned away my former self. . . .'

194

Yet nothing, in his days of success, became Falstaff so well as the dignity with which he accepted total failure. 'Master Shallow, I owe you a thousand pounds,' he merely threw out to the bewildered, disconsolate Justice; then, rapidly regaining his habitual poise: 'Sir, I will be as good as my word ... go with me to dinner. . . . I shall be sent for soon at night.'

Alas, Falstaff was never to be summoned. King Henry V was crowned King of England on April 9, 1413, at the age of 26; and thereafter Falstaff's existence was a slow decline. Temporarily he may have rallied. According to a Victorian critic, the ludicrous and ignominious episode described in *The Merry Wives of Windsor* illustrates 'the further degradation' of his personality caused by the young King's brutal treatment. Undoubtedly, it shows that he had lost his gift of charming: that he, who had so long mastered life, had begun to sink beneath the weight of years. The soldier, courtier, diplomatist, amorist was now the sport of provincial housewives, who crammed him into a basket of dirty clothes and tossed him 'hissing hot' into the Thames.

Falstaff's relations with women, however, were sufficiently complex to deserve a whole essay. During his prime, he was clearly a successful seducer, apt, as a gentleman born and bred – the denizens of the Boar's-Head always remembered his rank – to hold out specious hopes of marriage. Thus he had deluded 'old Mistress Ursula, whom I have weekly sworn to marry since I perceived the first white hair on my chin'. Thus, too, he exploited Mistress Quickly, the susceptible and good-natured innkeeper whom he had 'eaten out of house and home'. In his dealings with the opposite sex, Falstaff was usually a sound psychologist. He knew that Quickly, as a half-educated person, possessed an instinctive respect for any kind of written paper, and that, as one of nature's dupes, she had a fatal propensity for throwing good money after bad. Even more important, he knew that she adored him and, dazzled by his aristocratic panache, still had hopes of becoming Lady Falstaff.

He had already proposed, his victim reminded him – 'sitting in my Dolphin-chamber, at the round table, by a sea-coal fire, upon a Wednesday in Wheeson Week, when the Prince broke thy head ... thou didst swear to me then, as I was washing thy wound to marry me and make me my lady, thy wife'. And Falstaff had sealed the engagement by eliciting a loan of thirty shillings. Not only did Falstaff wave his debt aside: he had no difficulty in exacting a larger loan, though Quickly protested that, to find the money, she would be obliged to pawn her plate and strip the walls bare. Falstaff retorted, however, that both silver, or silver-gilt, goblets and 'these fly-bitten tapestries' had gone out of vogue: 'Let it be ten pound, if thou canst. Come, an 'twere not for thy humours, there's not a better wench in England. Go, wash thy face and draw the action.'

Much more genuine than his selfish and negligent affection for Quickly was Falstaff's passion for her gossip Doll. There is clearly some parallelism between his attachment to the Prince and the tragic story told in Shakespeare's *Sonnets*; and, if Prince Henry was his 'man right fair', Doll Tearsheet was his Dark Lady. The poet's beloved, the 'woman colour'd ill', may perhaps have been a London prostitute. Doll undoubtedly followed the same profession, and was infected by the occupational diseases of her trade. She 'burns poor souls,' Falstaff admitted wryly: 'burning' was a slang phrase for venereal infection.

Yet to Falstaff she personified youth itself; and, with Doll Tearsheet seated on his knee, this indomitably youthful adventurer felt, almost for the first time – he soon overcame and dismissed the sensation – the sudden chilly touch of old age:

'Thou dost give me flattering busses.'
'But my troth, I kiss thee with a most constant heart.'
'I am old, I am old.'
'I love thee better than I love e'er a scurvy young boy of them all.'
'What stuff wilt have a kirtle of? I shall receive money o' Thursday. ... A merry song: it grows late, we'll to bed. Thou'll forget me when I am gone.'

That last foreboding was unrealized: none of his onetime friends at the Boar's-Head ever succeeded in forgetting Falstaff. What then was the secret of his power and prestige? Partly, no doubt, his massive independence, his obstinate refusal either to accept the vainglorious jargon, or to embrace the conventions and superstitions, of his day. He lived in a period of war and political turmoil, amid 'iron men', soldiers and politicians, whose strenuous business was to 'make history'. Kingdoms must be saved or overthrown, battles fought and rebels vanquished. They were obsessed by Time; inflamed by the concept of Honour. Falstaff laughed at Honour, defied the ravages of Time, a one-man opposition who spoke for the Individual – and for the Individual's pleasures and privileges – against the collective tyranny of Law and Government. To virtue he did not pretend, though during early life, he asserted, he was 'as virtuously given as a gentleman need to be ... swore little ... went to a bawdy house not above once in a quarter,' even occasionally repaid the money that he borrowed. But Falstaff resolutely believed in happiness; and ordinary human happiness, then as now, was not a quality that politicians prized.

Of all the iron men, the worst was his former idol – Henry v, the so-called 'patriot king', who in 1415, on a trumped-up *casus belli*, launched his first bloody attack against the King of France. Leading the English armament were his mail-clad nobles. Supporting them, at a decent distance in the rear, marched Ancient Pistol, Corporal Nym and Lieutenant Bardolph, the latter soon to be hung for plundering a French church. One day, on the eve of departure, they assembled in a street near Eastcheap, Pistol flanked by Mistress Quickly, whom he had recently made his lawful wife – she was a conquest he had snatched from the arms of Nym – and whose modest fortune he was now enjoying.

There Falstaff's page overtook them, with news that his master, bedridden in his old quarters at the Boar's-Head, was now a very sick man. 'Ah, poor heart!' reported the hostess, having hurried to his side, 'he is so shaked of a burning quotidian tertian, that it is most lamentable to behold.' Falstaff's sickness was a malevolent fever, which during the course of the next few days slowly undermined his strength; and, when the Eastcheap gang again assembled, he had passed into a new existence.

'Would I were with him,' (cried loyal Bardolph) 'where some 'er he is, either in heaven or in hell!'

'Nay, sure, he's not in hell,' (replied the hostess). 'He's in Arthur's bosom, if ever man went to Arthur's bosom. A' made a finer end and went away an it had been any christom child; a' parted even just between twelve and one even at the turning o' the tide; for after I saw him fumble with the sheets, and play with flowers, and smile upon his fingers' ends, I knew there was but one way.... "How now, Sir John!" quoth I: "what, man, be o' good cheer." So a' cried out, "God, God, God!" three or four times. Now I, to comfort him, bid him, a' should not think of God; I hoped there was no need to trouble himself with any such thoughts yet. So a' bade me lay more clothes on his feet: I put my hand into the bed and felt them, and they were as cold as any stone, and so upward and upward, and all was as cold as any stone.'

Falstaff's last words were of 'green fields'; but during his delirium he had demanded sack, and – though this the hostess staunchly denied – he had also raved of women. When he expired, he was nearly seventy years old; and it is ironic that the devoted, ill-treated Quickly, so often the victim of his greed and opportunism, should have paid him a moving valedictory tribute. 'The King,' she exclaimed, 'has killed his heart.' Whatever else Sir John had lacked, he did not lack a capacity for generous emotion. In a world of callous, self-centred supermen and mean-spirited, self-seeking small men, only Falstaff had really loved and suffered: Falstaff alone had had a heart to break.

Date Due

DEC 18 '75			